SOUL
MATTERS

When you become aware of the deeper aspects of life and its' meaning, you begin to understand

SOUL MATTERS

A discussion of principles that will lead you to greater peace, deeper love, and enduring happiness.

AUSTIN VICKERS

COPYRIGHT © 2002 BY AUSTIN VICKERS

All rights reserved. No part of this book may be reproduced or utilized in any form or by any means, electronic or mechanical, including photocopying, recording, or by any information storage or retrieval system, without permission in writing from the Publisher.

ISBN 0-9714761-0-1

Library of Congress Control Number: 2001118983

FIRST EDITION

Printed in the United States of America

Book Design and layout by Madalyn Johnson

Not only am I indebted to you Madalyn for doing such a wonderful job with the presentation of my book, I am also grateful to you for allowing me to speak endlessly about my beliefs . . .
Thank you. I always enjoy our discussions of *soul matters*!

Back Cover photograph by Ernie Button

PUBLISHED BY QUANTUM HORIZONS BOOKS
A Division of Quantum Horizons, LLC.

**1730 E. WARNER ROAD
SUITE 10-142
TEMPE, ARIZONA 85284
480-491-5591**

To Christopher
Your enthusiasm and passion for life are a constant reminder to me of the value that life offers. Never be afraid to be that which you really are. I cherish your playful spirit, love, and friendship.
Know that I will always love you and be there for you...

To Danielle
Your sweet and gentle spirit reminds me what it is like to be in the presence of God. Do not forget to show yourself the same deep love you so easily give to others. I cherish your kindness, love, and insight. Know that our hearts will always beat as one...

To both of you
The daily business of our lives often makes it difficult to deeply share that which is in our hearts. I have often failed at communicating the depth of my admiration, appreciation and love for both of you, yet you have both always continued to love me unconditionally. I have at times miscommunicated my best intentions for you as criticism, and in the process may have contributed to a belief that you are somehow less than perfect. Yet you both continue to demonstrate the totality of the divinity from which you were created. I have stolen many moments that could have been spent with both of you to write the words contained in this book and learn the principles they embody, yet it is because of both of you that I did write them. For this I thank you. Words do not exist that are capable of adequately expressing how complete my life is, because you both are in it.

To mom and dad, my brother Michael, and the many people who have loved me and let me love them:

thank you for helping me see who I really am . . .

Contents

Part One. **Initial Perspective**

Part Two. **The Big Picture**

- *Life is a matter of perception.*
- *Past memories and future concerns should not be permitted to cloud the sunshine emitted from present moments.*
- *Life is a process of creation for which we alone are responsible.*
- *The summit of happiness is reached when a person is ready to be what she is.*

Part Three. **The Finer Details**

- *To become truly happy, you must simply do that which creates happiness.*
- *The Law of Self Realization – a formula for happiness.*

1. Balance

- *To be happy, you must be balanced. To be balanced, body, mind, and spirit must be carefully nurtured.*

2. Body

- *A healthy body is the surgical tool through which mind and spirit operate.*
- *Fruits of mind and flowers of spirit only flourish in healthy gardens.*
- *A gardener is a garden's way of taking care of itself.*
- *Air is the lifeblood of our bodily existence, without which the body cannot survive.*
- *Peace of mind and body are the states in which all growth occurs.*
- *Our bodies are communities in relationship with the earth.*
- *An active body facilitates an active mind and spirit.*
- *Nature is the living, visible garment of God.*

- Where you find joy and laughter, so too will you find a body that can heal itself.
- Music is the rhythm of spirit.
- The glory of the body is manifested through its senses.
- Sexual expression between two lovers is a glimpse of the divine union of mind, body, and spirit.
- In the end, our bodies are merely specific physical manifestations of the energy that exists in all life.

3. Mind

- We are thoughts that, through experience and evolution, have learned how to create a physical machine.
- Only those with ears can hear.
- Happiness requires the acceptance of responsibility.
- Make every thought and action a conscious choice.
- The happiest person is the person who has learned to be honest with himself.
- One of the greatest obstacles to mentally achieving happiness and love is judgment.
- Real satisfaction comes not from distraction, but rather from total awareness.
- Let passion and enthusiasm be what first come to mind when others think of you.
- Take it upon yourself from this moment onward to always look for and focus on the magic in life.
- Our dreams and our beliefs define the upper limits of what we can achieve.

4. Spirit

- When the body and mind are willing and able, the path is clear for spirit to emerge.
- We are not the body. We are not the mind. We are the ones who possess mind and body.
- The search for spirit must begin within.
- The true essence of God is not found in symbols that represent Her.
- The real nature of God is recognized by freedom of will and thought.
- Spiritual growth is an individual path.
- Let your light so shine that others can easily see God in you.

5. Expectation

- Life is most lived when attachment to result is lost.
- All of these things shall give thee experience.
- To be or not to be are equal parts of being.

6. Purpose

- The balance of body, mind, and spirit facilitates the focus of the soul toward purpose.
- Purpose of being can never be attained without the willingness to define and stand for what you believe.
- Intention never matures into purpose without realization through action.
- The greatest purpose of all is that which empowers and enriches the lives of others.

7. Love

- The truth about love is that love is our truth.
- The love we experience is directly proportionate to the degree in which we choose to see, and allow, love into our lives.
- Love's first requirement is that it be given to ourselves.
- Love and honesty are synonyms.
- There is no greater advice for you than that which lies within your own heart.
- How can I love me? Let me count the ways.
- The road to love of self is only blocked by us.
- I love because I choose to and want to, not because I need to.
- Love first!
- Love is not a limited resource, but rather is a well spring of unlimited supply.
- Loving relationships are the mirrors by which we see our shadows.
- Loving relationships will inevitably fail if they are not built upon complete honesty.
- To create a loving relationship, you must love yourself first.
- Relationships are the vehicles by which we manage the defining of our souls.
- True love makes no home for the ego.
- The real value of our lives is the measure by which we have learned to love.

Part Four.   **The End, The Beginning, The All**

- *The infinite strength of spirit and soul is the property of all.*
- *The true path to happiness and enlightenment is found by following your own heart, even if others do not follow or understand your direction.*
- *The Principles of Being.*

Part One.

Initial Perspective

My very first exposure to the strength of the human soul came when I was 19 years old. I had just moved to Chile, South America, to be a missionary and teach people about God. In retrospect, I knew very little about God or the soul, but what I lacked in knowledge I made up for in enthusiasm, innocence, and devotion.

As you might expect, I was rudely introduced to poverty – third world style – the very first day I arrived in Chile. This was not the lack-of-money-to-buy-what-one-wants kind of poverty. No, third world poverty is the complete lack of money to buy necessities like toilet paper, toothpaste, or soap. It is the lack of money to buy building materials to fix the holes in the tin roof of your shack so that, when it rains, your three children and your wife, who all sleep in the same bed, do not get wet. It is the lack of money to buy materials to build yourself a wooden outhouse so you and your family do not have to go to the bathroom behind your home where privacy can never be guaranteed. Third world poverty is the lack of resources to buy your family food on a daily basis.

In this kind of poverty, there are no shelters one can visit for cover from the elements. There are no soup kitchens where one can receive a hot meal, or a cold one for that matter. And there are no hospitals where one can obtain medicine if a family member is sick. There is practically nothing but faith that somehow, some way, you and your family will survive despite the circumstances.

No words can do justice to the sense of shock and dismay I felt the day I arrived from my warm, secure, middle class background to this existence. And nothing prepared me for what I found there, despite the horrific physical conditions.

Despite the lack of opportunity, despite the lack of shelter, medicine, and food, and despite the lack of hope in many cases, happiness and love were still abundant. I encountered many individuals who, despite the circumstances that they faced, still found a way to face the world every day with a smile for anyone who lifted their eyes to see, a tender word for someone else's equal misfortune, and love and service for those in need of a helping hand. It was here, amid poverty and misfortune, that I personally found happiness. Or at least it is where I began to understand what happiness is. It was in these surroundings that I first learned about real love, courage, faith, and responsibility, and the strength of the human soul. It was here that I was first exposed to the principles that would change my life.

I have since learned that certain principles are an instrumental part of true and enduring happiness and they form the basis for achieving the same no matter what our physical circumstances. These principles were equally available to me in the middle class life I left to become a missionary. I had only failed to recognize them as readily. I now know that it is not a change of environment that provides wisdom, although different experiences do give us greater perspective. However, I believe it is a willingness to learn and an openness to the promptings of the spirit and soul that ultimately lead to awareness, growth, and wisdom.

Some people believe they have to go to far away exotic lands and meet exotic people to satisfy the longings and needs of their soul. But they do not. The solution to our sense of emptiness, to our lack of vision, and to our lack of meaning, is found within us, not in some foreign land.

Since my return from Chile almost twenty years ago, I have seen the same qualities of courage, happiness, and love in the very wealthy, in the middle class, and in people from all walks of life. I believe I have been able to recognize these virtues in others because I learned to find them first within myself. I have also learned that people's qualities that we most often see and experience are, in fact, a reflection of that part of ourselves that we most often choose to experience.

Having found and elevated spiritual qualities and principles within myself has allowed me to see them more easily in others. In fact, it has radically changed the way I encounter the world. In large part, a world of fear has been replaced with one based on love. A world of hope and wonder has replaced a world of skepticism and cynicism. The change, of course, has not been with the world. I see now that the world has always remained the same. I am the one who has changed. I have learned that we can choose to have a different experience of the world than the one we have today. We can choose to experience the world through a different paradigm.

Every day we are presented with opportunities to define who we are, to decide whether we will love or not love, or whether we will act or react in compassion or fear. Fortunately, many of us are not faced with the kind of physical challenges and circumstances that make the emergence of these qualities difficult. But we all have our own challenges that present themselves each day and test our dedication and commitment to love, to being happy, and to becoming who we really are.

That is the real beauty and example of people like Jesus, Ghandi, Mother Theresa, and many other lesser-known people who have lived on this planet. They all refused to allow their circumstances or other people to take from them their God-like ability to love. In reaction to all things they consistently chose to be loving and caring. They chose to experience hope, love, and happiness in the face of adversity. They chose to follow the whispers of their souls and dared to become who they really were. In so doing, they found meaning, peace, and great authentic power.

The greatest message we have from these "soul travelers" is the choice they made to be living examples of the principles they espoused. Take for example the life of Jesus. Regardless of our choice of religion, one of the greatest things about this man was that he refused to be anything other than the greatest vision he must have had of himself. He refused to stop loving and giving to people even in light of the intense persecution that ultimately led to his crucifixion. He refused to compromise his passion and purpose for a life of complacency, despite the pain he knew he would suffer and the difficult challenges that he would face. Jesus' great power, his capacity to love, changed the world. And it his name, and the names of people like Mohammed, and Buddha, and other individuals who shared Jesus' ability to love, that people remember, honor, and worship. By their lives, we learn that love truly is the greatest and most enduring power that exists on earth.

There are modern day examples, as well, of great love and compassion. Not long ago I read a newspaper story that struck me as an unusual example of compassion in a world that seems, at times, to largely ignore such a virtue. The story did not make the headlines, nor was it extensive. Rather, it was a small caption that simply stated the following:

"Norbert Reinhart, Chief Executive of Ontario, Canada-based Grey Star Resources was freed [in Columbia] after three months as a hostage. He had offered himself in exchange for an employee, Ed Leonard, whom he had never met . . . ." What an extraordinary event! In a world where so many have forgotten how to love and care for others, we find a gem. An example of someone who was willing to put his own life into peril to save the life of an employee he had never met!

It is sometimes difficult to comprehend the immense loving actions of some people. What is it that gives some people the ability to love unconditionally? What values or traits are possessed by those who choose love and compassion in response to any circumstance, no matter how difficult or challenging? Is it a learned behavior or is it innate? What is it that allows some people to react to any situation with a positive attitude, while others seemingly cannot help but be negative? How can we be truly happy in the face of so much tragedy, so much unloving behavior around us? How and why should we follow what our souls would have us do? Where do we find inner peace and tranquility?

This book attempts to answer these questions through the premise that life, love, and happiness are choices. You are today only that which you chose yesterday to become, either consciously or unconsciously. You are not who others think you are; you are not who you have been; and you are not who you think you have to be. You **are** simply who you **choose to be** and how you **choose to love** today, either consciously or unconsciously.

To be truly happy, to react positively to negative situations, and to choose love and compassion in reaction to all events and people, you must learn to recreate yourself within parameters that you alone decide. Too often, our lives are defined by what others expect of us. In trying to please others, like our parents, teachers, and friends, we soon find ourselves living a life that pleases everyone but ourselves. Unhappiness and unloving behavior is often the result.

This is a book about learning how to be who you really are; how to recreate yourself; how to become happy; and how to love in action and reaction to all things. In essence, it is the advocacy of a new model of thinking designed to create lasting happiness. It is my view of principles that enhance our experience of the soul. In other words, it is a discussion of "soul matters." By no means is it complete, nor does it claim to be. Rather, it simply is a discussion of some "principles of being" that help form the creation of deep and meaningful happiness in our lives.

Soul Matters begins with a very general overview, what I call the Big Picture, of happiness. It discusses principles like perspective, responsibility, and present-moment focus, and aims to help the reader understand these principles as facilitators that begin to center awareness on the self. Awareness is the first step towards realization, and the first few chapters begin by helping the reader create a frame of mind where cognizance of happiness, and the change required to obtain it, can begin.

The book then proceeds to a discussion entitled the Finer Details. At the outset of these chapters the reader is introduced to a simple formula – one that I call the Law of Self Realization. This law is designed to give the reader a simple way of remembering some fundamental principles that form a solid foundation for a deeper understanding of the soul. It shows how this understanding, when put in practice, leads to the creation of happiness. In the chapters that follow, the principles that constitute this formula are explored and defined and their correlation to happiness is explained. It is within this section that the reader is exposed to the importance of focus on the body, mind and spirit and the need for the balance of each.

In the next section, purpose is defined and illustrated to show how it provides meaning to life. In this section, the reader is challenged to think about that aspect of life that will provide him or her with purpose as well as a greater sense of their own divinity, and how they might incorporate the pursuit of this purpose into their lives.

Expectation, attachment, and judgment, what I believe are the three deadly sins, are discussed next. This section explains how each of these traits is a function of fear, and how each attempts to mediate our insecurities through a false elevation of self that leads to unhappiness. The reader is shown how coming to terms with these socially-infused traits can significantly contribute to a sense of happiness and peaceful existence in his or her own life.

The remainder of the book is dedicated to a discussion of what is perhaps the most important principle of all – the one that not only is essential for happiness – but also is essential for life itself, for out of it, all life is created. It is the very essence of soul. This is the principle of love.

Finally, the conclusion summarizes the principles found in the Law of Self Realization into a document I call the "Principles of Being." In learning to live these principles, I believe, happiness and "soul-full living" become inevitable conclusions. These "Principles of Being" are what I hope to become. They are the principles that I believe in, and they are my passion. They are an example of a path to happiness and the soul that is created through the divine gifts of experience, intellect, heart and spirit. They are a declaration of the principles upon which I believe true happiness is constructed, despite the conditions and change that so often beset our modern lives.

The hardest thing I have found in writing a book such as this is trying to capture in fixed form what tends to be fluid and evolving. If we are open-minded and aware, then learning never ceases. It only deepens, grows and develops. I am the first to admit the severity with which my beliefs have changed over time. I know now, however, that my prior beliefs served a grand and divine purpose – they led me to the path I am on today.

I assume that my beliefs and "truths" will continue to evolve over time, as I am more committed to the discovery, awareness, and learning of truth and wisdom than I am committed to the need to be right. Thus I find it difficult to profess to teach universal truths. I am open to the possibility that I may yet evolve to a different understanding about these or any other principles.

Even during the writing of this book I found my perspective changing. Perhaps, if I were to begin this work again today, it might read different from what is presented here. That is because my understanding of "soul matters," even since the writing of this book, has deepened. Today, I enjoy a new and even deeper understanding of some of the principles contained herein and I hope to write further about that fuller understanding someday. Thus, this work does not represent the end of my learning, but rather the beginning.

As learning is a progression for all, I believe this work has value for any that will take the time to study it. It is not meant to dictate principles that are – but rather is meant to suggest principles that can be. It is, if you allow it to be, an illustration of one of many paths to a deeper understanding of the soul and to creating happiness in life.

This book was written on the premise that "soul matters" more than anything in life. As such, it is written in an attempt to touch you at a spiritual or soul level. It aims to inspire you to understand that your life is a process of creation, and not just a process of reaction.

The key to these changes lies not in the pages of this book, but, rather, lies inside you. The thoughts and words contained herein are designed only to provoke your own thoughts and words, and to help you discover **your truth**. It is only from this process that action will spring forth, and only through action that realization of **your truth** can be attained. Your life is the tool by which this truth is created and developed.

There comes a period in many of our lives when we seemingly lose recognition of the value of "soul matters," and pursuing our truth and passion. For many, perhaps, this recognition was never there to begin with. For others, we lose our siren call somewhere along the way in a life often marked by a concession of the principles and passions we once held dear.

In our culture it is easy to become lost. So much of what is being written for us, produced through visual mediums, and emulated in our work and community environments seems more focused on entertaining or controlling us, rather than on teaching and inspiring us. It is not that these mediums do not have socially redeeming values. To be clear they do, for they are an equal aspect of our collective soul.

However, we seem to seek refuge in these mediums as a means of escaping our reality, rather than searching that reality for principles that elevate and inspire us. We seem to want to avoid the pain and challenges that come from soul searching and following our passions, in favor of pursuing pleasure distractions or simply coping with circumstances we do not understand we have created.

The writer and philosopher Thomas Moore said: "The great malady of the twentieth century, implicated in all of our troubles and affecting us individually and socially, is 'loss of soul.' When soul is neglected, it doesn't just go away; it appears symptomatically in obsessions, addictions, violence, and loss of meaning. Our temptation is to isolate these symptoms or to try to eradicate them one by one; but the root problem is that we have lost our wisdom about the soul, even our interest in it."

It is my observation, however, that we are beginning to witness a renewed sense of interest in "soul matters," in pursuing truth, and in finding meaning and happiness in our lives. We are looking, increasingly, to elevate our souls. Every day I see more examples of individuals who refuse to compromise, who refuse to simply be entertained and occupied in the face of unfulfilled purpose. These individuals are pursuing their passions and insisting on their right to pursue a deeper and more meaningful existence. They are unwilling to accept a life of lesser happiness and meaning. We are experiencing a rapidly growing awareness and thirst for fundamental truths about the soul. Countless numbers of books are being written about the meaning of life and principles that teach us to examine introspectively our hearts, minds, and souls. And yet, we do not have enough written and spoken on such "soul matters."

We must continue to allow this fire of learning to consume us. We must allow it to transform our lives and our relationships. It must become everything to us, for indeed all else is illusion. The daily busyness of our lives is simply a refiners' fire by which the layers of this illusion are slowly burned away.

We must consent individually, and as a community, to the elevation of soul that comes from learning these principles in whatever form they are taught. We must let go of the fear of change, disruption, and confusion that often blocks this teaching and learning from occurring. We must remember that it is from the chaos of confusion and change, not the comfort of stability and constancy that wisdom most often emerges.

We are seeing a resurgence of principles and teachings intended to take our spirits to greater heights. Successful teaching takes the soul to greater heights when it provides its listeners with guiding principles, values, and solutions for dealing with the frailties of the human mind and experience. On rare occasions, when inspiration, creativity and purpose conspire, certain teachings, told in just the right way, alter and change our lives forever. They do so because they provide us with an association to wisdom, love and divinity, and they help us to create our own paths for achieving the same.

It is to this end that I have written this book. It is my desire, my hope, and my prayer that this book will change your life in the same way that learning these principles has changed mine.

- The Author

Part Two.

The Big Picture

AUSTIN VICKERS

1.

Life is a matter of perception.

Imagine a situation where you are traveling on a plane and carrying a luggage bag that you place below your seat. In one of the cases you have a bag of your favorite candy, a bag of M&M's, which you like to carry on long trips. After lunch, and before you take a nap, you like to indulge in your candy.

The plane is full and you find yourself sitting next to another passenger. You do not really have much discussion with him, other than the usual pleasantries. After lunch, however, the strangest thing happens. The man reaches under your seat and removes your bag of M&M's. He slowly opens the bag, pours himself a handful, and then places the bag back under your seat.

How would you feel at this point? Would you be angry, upset, or bothered? Like most people, you would probably be quite amazed at his brashness.

Your amazement soon turns to shock, however, as he reaches down again and takes more of your M&M's. So you reach down, retrieve the bag of M&M's, and pour yourself a handful. The man smiles at you. Before long, the two of you are munching away, each taking turns eating from the bag of M&M's. Neither you, nor he speaks to each other, but each is conscious of the others' actions. Finally, he reaches down and grabs the remainder of the bag of M&M's. He pours himself the last handful and eats them.

Now how would you feel? Undoubtedly, you are somewhat surprised by the audacity of this passenger and, perhaps, you are a little or a lot upset that he has helped himself to so much of your candy, even eating the last of it.

The flight ends and both of you go your separate ways. You are left pondering how rude some people are capable of being as you walk off the plane. When you get to the baggage handling area you reach into your case to get the tickets that correspond to your luggage. To your surprise you find inside your case an unopened bag of M&M's, the one that you originally brought onto the plane.

In an instant you begin to blush as you realize the mistake you have made. It was not your bag of M&M's that you were both eating, but rather a bag belonging to the fellow passenger.

Now how would you feel? Embarrassed for sure. But how would you feel towards the passenger who sat next to you? He quietly shared his bag of M&M's with you and said nothing as you aggressively tried to eat as much as he was eating, under the assumption that he was eating your candy. If you are like most people, the feelings of dismay, frustration, and disbelief that you would have had before would be quickly replaced with feelings of humility, embarrassment, and probably some regard towards this stranger who had been so kind to share with you.

This is a paradigm shift, a fundamental change of perception based on the discovery of new facts. It has the potential to greatly alter your perspective, in a matter of seconds, once new facts are introduced into the picture.

From a big picture perspective, it is important to understand that your view of life is simply one grand paradigm. It is a perception, just one view of events, circumstances and people. You do not have the absolute truth about anything because, like the story above, you do not have all of the facts. You only have your own perception of the events that transpire within this paradigm.

The intent of this book is to create a paradigm shift in you that will open your eyes to a more spectacular view of the world and your life. It will do so, by hopefully providing you with some tools to discover other "facts," which are likely to change the paradigm through which you have seen the world thus far.

There are many people who do not challenge their own perceptions; they believe their view of the world is the absolute truth. They make assumptions about everything and rarely, if ever, stop to consider that they may be completely wrong. Often their viewpoints are narrow and they are blind to the discovery of other facts that perhaps could change their perception, or alter their paradigm.

Every person has a different experience of life. Since it is only through our own experience that we are capable of viewing the actions of others, we can never determine the absolute truth or reality for them. While sometimes we reach a point in our lives where we feel passionately about the things we believe in, do not forget that such beliefs can change. When given new facts, like in our example above, we are forced to change our views, unless we refuse to be open-minded. Inevitably our views, opinions, and perceptions are extremely limited and rarely are true for others, because they are based on our experience, not theirs. And our experience changes over time.

Individual beliefs are never right or wrong. Rather, they are simply reflections of an individual's experience. That is why beliefs are as varied as are experiences. Be careful, therefore, in being too zealous about what you believe.

You have formed your beliefs from the teachings and modeling of parents, teachers, friends and others. Interacting with them, you have acquired their thoughts, words and actions and correlated them with your own experiences. Typically, when their behavior or words are consistent with your experiences, you judge them to be good or right. When their behavior or words contradict your own experiences, you may judge them to be bad or wrong, unless they trigger a change in you. Sometimes, we see behavior, or we hear words that accord with a change that we are experiencing. These behaviors or words, then, often form the catalyst for our personal change. In any case, however, remember that although your beliefs are a reflection of who you are today, they may not reflect who you may be tomorrow. Your experience may change and your teachers may change as well.

Do not fear change. Do not fear new or different teachings or beliefs. Be open to the possibility that they may have more relative truth for you today than do your existing beliefs and values. Try to assess them from a position of how they can positively affect your life and the lives of others, rather than from a point of comparison to your existing beliefs. Consume new facts, information and values with the hunger of a starving man. Allow yourself to consider them and, potentially, accept them as true for you, even if it means rejecting previously held beliefs. The more open you are to the potential for change and growth via a paradigm shift, the greater and more credible the values and beliefs will be that you ultimately choose to represent yourself.

Above all, remember that the glasses through which you view life are different from mine. You should expect, therefore, that your view of life will be different from mine; it is based on a different perception and a different paradigm. But that difference should never be mistaken for error, confusion or chaos.

God is, in fact, the inspiration behind all relative truth, despite differences and apparent contradictions. The differences, you see, are temporal and are not as they appear. They are not real. They are merely part of a grand illusion in which we all participate. The contradictions that we see come merely from the same truth adapting itself to the varying circumstances of different experiences. It is always the same light, it just appears different depending upon the color of the lenses through which it shines.

Take for example misery. Misery comes only from perception. It is not caused by conditions or by external forces. Many people will say that they are miserable because of this thing or that. The blame for their misery is almost always placed on external objects or factors. Acknowledgment is rarely given to the fact that misery is only a perception that is created by the perceiver. The fire that cooks your meal can also burn your child. If it does the latter, it is never the fault of the fire. Fire is just fire, wind is just wind, water is just water, and fear is just fear. It is what we do with these things and how we perceive and react to them that causes misery.

If you drown yourself in water then you may be a fool. If you use the water, however, to satisfy your thirst or clean your wounds, then you are probably wise. External things are never good or bad and never **cause** us misery or happiness. Rather, it is how we perceive, react to, and use them for our experience that determines whether we are miserable or happy. We, alone, have the ability to control those perceptions and reactions.

When you begin to realize that your view of life or of any thing, event or circumstance is merely one of many possible perceptions, then you begin to become less judgmental of whether the object of your judgment is good or bad, right or wrong. You begin to realize that many things, indeed most things, simply just are.

Like the M&M example, judgment of any event, person or thing in your life is premature and foolish unless you have all the facts . . . and you never have all of the facts. So how can you judge anything? To understand the big picture, you must first realize that everything in life is a matter of perception. Your perception is not the ultimate truth or reality, it is simply a limited view of any one thing.

2.

Past memories and future concerns should not be permitted to cloud the sunshine that is emitted from present moments. Every moment of your existence is an opportunity for you to enjoy, appreciate, and love the life that is unfolding before you.

Lasting happiness, for many people, is like trying to discover the origins of the universe and our existence: it is something sought, but never obtained. Despite all their efforts to search for lasting happiness, it remains elusive. As a result, pleasure often becomes a replacement for happiness, distracting the seeker from one moment to the next. These pleasure distractions, however, never replace true happiness and they ultimately leave one feeling unfulfilled and unhappy.

True happiness, however, is not beyond our reach. Its resting place has been known for thousands of years, and is discussed consistently by all great thinkers, philosophers and "soul teachers." True happiness, it is taught, is within us. It comes from a search within.

Happiness is a voluntary state of well-being; in essence it is a choice. Every moment we choose the state of our well-being by choosing our reaction to the circumstances at hand, whether we do so knowingly or unknowingly. That is the real difference between people who are happy and those that are not. Those that are happy understand that their happiness is a choice and they are conscious of their choice. Unhappy people do not realize that they are in fact choosing to be unhappy, for they do so unconsciously.

Happiness is created. It is a learned behavior, a habit if you will. It remains elusive for many of us because we have never really learned how to foster it within ourselves. Few people teach us how to be truly happy. Few courses in school provide instruction on how to be whole, how to love, and how to be happy. Yet is there anything more important in our lives? Is there any thing that helps us more to be productive, contributing members of society than when we are happy?

Happiness is one of the most important attributes of human behavior we can attain. For when we are happy with ourselves, when we love and accept ourselves, we become free to share our happiness and love with others. When we are forever chasing happiness, but never finding it, our lives become frustrated and this frustration overshadows our ability to give love to others.

We need to start creating our own happiness today. And I literally mean today for happiness does not exist either in the past or in the future. True happiness can only be created by a focus on the present moment. A memory of past happiness is, in reality, a pleasurable moment that distracts us from the present. Thoughts of a happy tomorrow are in fact dreams that provide an escape from the present. True and lasting happiness is a state of well-being that is created in the present moment.

"When I dance, I dance. When I eat, I eat." The French philosopher Montaigne wrote these words with the message that we should be present-moment focused. To borrow a phrase from the computer industry, I call it "**real time**." In the computer world real time is live time, an instantaneous recording and playback of the moment. If your thoughts are spent worrying about past failures or mistakes, or they are spent contemplating the future - you are losing **real time**.

John Lennon once said: "Life is what happens while you are making other plans." In our lives, the only **real time** is what is happening right now - present moment. It is the only time that really matters. So many of us, whether we are in a certain place, with certain people, or in a certain moment of time, are in fact not there. We are lost somewhere else thinking about the past or contemplating what will happen in the future. Meanwhile, the subtle sweet nuances of the present moments are missed. The laughter of a child, the song of a bird, or the smile that radiates warmth – are often lost because they are not noticed, nor fully appreciated.

Thoughts of past and future remove from our gaze the unfolding beauty of the present.

I like to say that happiness in life is like a raffle – you must be present to win. Live in the moment now. Begin to have present-sense awareness. What is happening right now? Is it raining or is the sun shining? If it is raining, pay close attention to the rain and try to appreciate the nourishment it is bringing to the earth. If the sun is shining, feel the warmth on your skin. Focus on its radiance and find the unique shadows that it produces. What are people around you doing? Focus on those that are laughing or who are happy and allow their happiness to affect you. What is your body doing? How does it feel? Begin to use all of your senses to appreciate what is happening now.

Focus upon what you see, hear, touch, smell and sense in this exact moment. This present-sense awareness is **real time**. When you begin to fill your life with **real time**, you will waste less time worrying about the past or the future. More importantly, you will begin to value the present moment and will fill it with thoughts, words, and actions that stimulate your senses and inspire and uplift you. Open your senses to this moment and you will begin to consciously experience the full impact of life itself. You cannot give a greater gift of life than this to yourself.

Once we begin to focus on present-sense awareness and fill our lives with **real time**, we will discover an entirely new world commanding our attention. We will no longer respond only to obvious assaults on our senses, but we will begin to take notice of and pay attention to more subtle contacts. Whether it is the sounds of a gentle stream far away, the sounds of children laughing at a playground around the corner, or simply the internal sounds of your body, **real time** demands our attention to what is happening now.

From this focus, new intentions will form in our lives. These intentions will be centered on that which is real and defined in the present-moment. Unlike our intentions of the past, they will not be based on worry or fear, but on an appreciation for what is happening now. That is because worry and fear are creatures of the future, not the present.

Fear is a learned response. Children are not afraid until they learn to be afraid. They do not fear anything until we teach them to do so, by word or example. We teach our children to fear the unknown. Ultimately, most of our fear is fear of the unexplained or unfamiliar, which is why our fear is rarely centered in the present moment. Fear usually arises when we leave the present and begin to focus on the past or contemplate the possible future. When we think about the past or speculate about the future, however, we rarely engage all of our senses. Thus, we create more room for emotion and inevitably fear finds its way in.

Even when we are experiencing a moment that is causing us intense pain, be it emotional or physical, fear rarely arises in that moment but rather it comes later when we remember the moment or when we imagine similar moments reoccurring. It is then that our fears arise. Present-moment focus, however, does not allow room for fear because in the present-moment more of our senses our engaged. We can smell, taste, hear, see, and feel the very moment we are in. There is little room for fear. Thus, to help avoid living in fear, we must begin to focus on the present.

To achieve true and lasting happiness, we must live our lives in **real-time**. Each and every day we must begin to consciously force ourselves to live, think, and feel in the present moment, not in the past or the future. To do this successfully, it takes effort and practice. As you think about this concept each day, stop whenever you can and try to engage all of your senses. Identify out loud to yourself or your companion what each of your senses is noticing at that given moment. This practice will help you become more present moment focused in your life. As you become more present-moment focused, you will worry less and your life will begin to feel more enriched. This will lead to a greater sense of appreciation and gratitude, and ultimately more happiness, as these things are important components of happiness.

Appreciating is recognizing. It is present-sense awareness. It is **real time**. Appreciation is a universal force that brings to those that exercise it more of that which is being appreciated, which in turn breeds more happiness. The processes of appreciation, gratitude and present-sense awareness ultimately form a spiral of positive feelings that will lift your spirit higher and higher.

3.

Life is a process of creation for which we alone are responsible.

It was once said that you better enjoy the road you are on for it will take you to where it is going. I say that we should enjoy the life we have for it is the one we have created. While it is easy to think that conditions in life happen to us, rather than because of us, such thinking is misguided. The specifics of our lives today are the consequences of our choices, conscious or unconscious, of yesterday.

Take for example our careers or our relationships. They only ever ultimately fail because we allow them to. We are the ones that stop taking the interest in them, or making the efforts necessary to enhance them. While at first we may enjoy them unconditionally, over time we begin to focus on their negatives and we begin to look more selfishly at what we receive from them. Soon we find that our partners share in our discontent, or things happen in our employment that lead to our departure.

It is important to recognize that our thoughts and intentions have power, and whether we act upon them or not, they can independently lead to change. Thus, the circumstances in our lives are the consequences, not only of our actions, but also of our thoughts and intentions. We should begin to examine our circumstances, especially those we are not happy with, to better understand their relationship to our choices and our intentions. Developing this understanding is important as it ultimately provides the keys for changing those conditions we believe do not represent who we are or want to be.

Viktor Frankl, the Jewish psychiatrist who was imprisoned by the Germans during WWII, wrote: "We who lived in the concentration camps can remember those who walked through the huts comforting others, giving away their last piece of bread. They may have been few in number, but they offer sufficient proof that everything can be taken from a human being but one thing – the last of our freedoms – to choose our spirit in any given set of circumstances."

It is easy at times to look at our lives and the actions of others that affect us and believe that we are being acted upon. That someone else is responsible for our state of being. But the truth of the matter is that, along the way, we contributed to that state. Perhaps our action was simply inaction – failing to take proactive steps to change an event. Nevertheless, it is important that we take responsibility for our inactions and that we see the way they contribute to the present. Only then do we become empowered to change and to take positive action that will lead to the results we want in life.

Every thing in our lives can be analyzed in this objective way. We can all think of changes we might have made that would have altered our present course. This kind of analysis, however, should not be used for the purpose of blaming ourselves, or for feeling self-pity. Rather, we should do it solely to acknowledge that we are ultimately responsible for our lives and our state of being. Once we recognize this, we become free to escape the bondage of victimization.

As long as you believe you are a victim of other people or of your circumstances, then you are likely to feel there is little or nothing you can do to escape them. However, the minute you acknowledge your own role in your circumstances, then you become free to acknowledge the power and choice you have to change them.

But you might say, "Sometimes the actions of others make me so angry, or they disappoint or depress me." Or you might say, "I did not do anything, they did. So it is their fault that I am angry or depressed or upset." Do not be a slave to your senses or emotions. Understand that emotional responses are not beyond your control. Even if you typically react to a specific situation a certain way, it does not mean you **must** react that way. It only means that you are **programmed** to react a particular way.

You can change your programming and react differently. Programmed reactions are an unconscious consequence of perception and learned behavior. As children, we learn through the examples of our parents and friends and peers, when we should react in anger, jealousy, frustration or some other negative emotion. We receive a form of validation when we react in these ways, whether it is pity, concern, or simply attention, and soon the reactions are programmed. By learning to be conscious of your reactions and your perceptions, and by understanding your role in creating them, you can begin to change them. You can begin to make conscious choices that reflect who you want to be, rather than submit to unconscious reactions that feel outside of your control.

Learn to become a master of yourself and to view negative circumstances and people as teachers who can show you ways to improve and empower yourself. Strive to choose loving and peaceful reactions to every situation and person that challenges you, and your internal power will grow infinitely.

Every day, in every circumstance in which you find yourself, you choose the life you experience. If you are unhappy, it is because you are choosing unhappiness by making decisions that do not reflect what is really important to you, or that do not reflect who you really are or want to be. If you are unhappy more than you care to be, instead of blaming other people or circumstances for your misery, decide instead to understand your contribution to the misery and alter your reactions and choices. Decide to become a master of yourself, rather than try, like most, to become a master of life's events.

Achieving true and total happiness is not, and will never be, dependent upon your circumstances or any change in them. Circumstances do not, and cannot, guarantee happiness. We may choose to be happier when our circumstances change and we perceive that change to be for the better. We must be clear, however, that the new conditions did not cause our newly discovered happiness. Rather, we simply chose to react more positively to them. Thus, achieving true and total happiness only comes from changing our attitudes and perceptions, and by finding the beauty, peace and happiness within life as it is.

Richard Carlson, a noted author in the field of personal improvement, once said: "The truth is, there's no better time to be happy than right now. If not now, when? Your life will always be filled with challenges. It's best to admit this to yourself and decide to be happy anyway." Happiness truly is a decision to find in any event or person the gifts offered for our own growth and development. I like to call this way of looking at life "success orientation."

Some people may criticize this philosophy as being "pollyanna," or not being realistic about life. But what is realistic? What is real? Are the negative aspects of life more real than the positive ones? Reality is relative. Negative elements of life are only created by my reaction to and my acceptance of anything as negative. If I do not accept or acknowledge them as negative, then they can have no negative affect on me.

Positive elements that I recognize in all things enrich my life and fill me with appreciation, gratitude and hope. What is more real than this? When you learn to be success oriented, you attract successful results and successful people. Your positive energy becomes infectious and all that is successful is drawn to you. Focus on, expect and appreciate success and life will respond to you by providing more of it.

4.

"The summit of happiness is reached,
when a person is ready to be what he is"

- Erasmus

In your journey of recreation, you must be yourself and be willing to relinquish the opinions of others. The only opinion that really matters is the one you have of yourself. It is this opinion that forms the limits of your achievements and potential. To be truly happy, it is essential to be yourself and stop the quest for the approval of others. The following story is a good example of this:

Stiff as the icicles in their beards, the Ice Kings sat in the great hall and stared at Thor who had lumbered to the far north to stagger them with his gifts, which back home seemed scarcely human. Throughout the preliminary bragging, Zeur, his sideman, reeled off Thor's accomplishments, fit for sagas or a seat on the bench of the Gods.

With a sliver of his beard an Ice King picked his teeth, "is he a drinker?"

Zeur boasted of challengers laid out as cold as pickled herrings. The Ice King offered a horn-cup, as long as a harp's neck, full of mead.

Thor braced himself from elbow to belly and tipped the cup, drinking as deep as he could, then deeper, till his broad belt buckled. He had quaffed one inch.

"Maybe he is better at something else," and Ice King muttered, yawning.

Remembering the boulders he had seen Thor heave and toss in the pitch of anger, Zeur proposed a bout of lifting weights.

"You men have been hewing rocks from here to there for ages," and Ice King said. "They cut no ice. Lift something harder." He whistled and out came a grey-green cat with cold, mousy eyes. Thor gave it a pat, then thrust his heavy hands under it, stooped, heisted, heisted again, turned red in the face, bit his lip, and heisted again from the bottom of his heart – all he could lift was one limp forepaw.

Now pink in the face himself, Zeur said quickly that heroes can have bad days, like all people, but Thor of all the mortals was the most accomplished wrestler and would stake his Godhood on one fall.

Seeming too bored to bother, and Ice King waved his chilly fingers around the hall saying, "Does anyone need some trifling exercise before we go glacier-carving in the morning?" An old woman hobbled in, foul-faced and gamy, as bent in the back as any female of burden, as grey as water, and as feeble as an oyster. An Ice King said, "She's thrown some boys in her time."

Thor would have left, insulted, but Zeur whispered, "When the word gets south, she'll be at least an Ogress." Thor reached out sullenly and grabbed her elbow, but she quick-slivered him and grinned her gums. Thor tried his patented hammerlock takedown, but she melted away like steam from a leaky sauna. He tried a whole-nelson - it shrank to half, to a quarter, and then to nothing. He stood there, panting. "Who got me into this test of godliness?" he asked. Just then, as fast as lightening, the woman belted Thor with her bony fist and boomed him to one knee, but fell to her own knee, as pale as moonlight.

Unable to lift his head because of shame, Thor left by the back door, refusing to be consoled by Zeur's plans for a quick revision of the evening's events. He went back South, tasting his bitter lesson moment by moment. For the rest of his life he believed himself a pushover, faking greatness along a tawdry string of misadventures.

Meanwhile, the Ice Kings trembled in their chairs . . . but not from the cold. They had seen a mortal man hoist high the great horn-cup that ends deep in the ocean and lower all seven seas by his own stature; they had seen him move the cat of the world, hefting the pillar of one paw, the entire northern hemisphere; they had seen a mere mortal wrestle with death herself and match her knee for knee, grunting like thunder.

No, the Ice Kings did not tremble because of the cold. They trembled because for thousands of years they had easily controlled and manipulated mortals without fear of recourse. In Thor, however, they saw for the first time that man was close to obtaining their godly powers. They were only able to destroy Thor, not because he lacked the powers that they possessed, but because he failed to see them in himself.

Deepak Chopra, the noted author and "life teacher," once said: "To be unattached means that you are free from outside influences that overshadow your real self. The paradox is that to get the most passion from life, you must be able to stand back and be yourself. Passion and commitment, love and dedication, self-worth and fulfillment blossom when you are free from narrow attachments."

Many people seem to live their lives in anticipation of the few minutes of approval they receive on occasions when they interact with family, friends or associates. They pursue a certain career, take a certain job, date or marry a certain person, or act in a particular way because those actions meet the approval of someone else in their lives. Or perhaps, they avoid a course of action because it is generally not accepted as the "thing to do" by family or friends.

Unless your actions truly make you happy, that is unless they define who it is you are and want to be, actions taken for the approval of others will leave you feeling unsatisfied and unhappy. If you are living life for others, and not yourself, you will be sacrificing too much for an amount of approval that will never be sufficient. You cannot avoid unhappiness this way.

To become truly happy and at peace, you must learn to stand back and be yourself. You must learn to free yourself from the outside influences that overshadow your real self, and learn to rid yourself of attachment to outside approval. The only approval that matters, that can generate true happiness, is the approval of self. Approval of self is manifested, not by saying or thinking that you like yourself, but by taking the risk to be yourself, even in the face of opposition from family and friends.

When we begin to lose unnecessary attachment to the

approval of others, we become more willing to take risks. Not risks that put us, or others, in danger, but risks that deep down we yearn to take. These risks may include upsetting others who would have us live our lives differently than we want to live them.

To become truly happy and to connect with our souls, we must be willing to take the risk of being, that is manifesting publicly, who we really are. Why is this risk important? Because taking risks allows us to experience new things, new reactions and new perceptions. Through this experience, we are better able to understand and define ourselves.

All choices and actions involve risk. When we laugh out loud, we risk appearing foolish. When we cry in public, we risk appearing sentimental and weak. When we reach out for relationships, we risk involvement with complications. When we expose our feelings, we risk exposing our true selves and having others reject who we are. When we speak about our ideas, dreams, and hopes before others, we risk ridicule. When we live we risk death. When we hope for things, we risk despair at their non-fulfillment. When we try to achieve, we risk failure. And when we love, we risk not being loved in return.

The person who is unwilling to risk manifests that they are not comfortable with who they really are. The person who does not risk unconsciously acknowledges that they are controlled by their fears. The person who will not risk cannot experience. The person who does not experience does not live, does not grow and does not develop. Risks must be taken, though, for it is through risks that we learn to live and love ourselves.

We have a lot to overcome to realize our fullest potential and be truly happy. Unfortunately, many of us have been taught all of our lives that we are weak, inherently sinful, less than perfect, and that our standing in life is dependent upon our acceptance by God or others. These ideas are reinforced every time we are criticized, belittled, or corrected. These notions are strengthened every time we have been shown that, to make someone else happy, we must be different than how we are.

Criticism, correction and belittling by parents, teachers and friends unknowingly teach us that we are somehow less than whole, that we are not good enough as we are. Ultimately, to win back their approval we are expected to change or alter our behavior, to be something different from how we are. Thus, we are taught a process of seeking approval from others. This process robs us of self-worth, independence and free will. It robs us of the right and privilege to feel good about how we are, even if that is different from how others would like us to be. It is a process that forces us to be dependent on the approval of others to be happy.

We are, in fact, created perfectly. We are neither bad nor sinful, and we are not created to prove our worthiness to God or be accepted by others. We are already worthy of God's presence. We are created out of God. We are created to learn to who we really are. We are created to manifest our godliness and individuality. We are created to experience and from this experience, to define ourselves. We will always be accepted into the presence of God, for God's love is unconditional. It is pure love. We have no reason to feel shame, and no reason to feel guilt. We do not need anyone else to realize our fullest potential. We are independent and free to realize our own hopes and dreams. We are free to be who we really are. We must begin to value our differences and recognize our true worth as individual manifestations of divinity.

The person who is ready to be herself, is the person who loves herself. She is the person who accepts her differences from others, indeed who values those differences, despite the difficulty others may choose to experience in response to those differences. She is the person who no longer seeks the approval of others, but rather, who understands the importance and the need to demonstrate self-approval. She is the person who eagerly and willingly follows the dictates of her own heart. She is the person who has learned to rid herself of attachment to the opinions and acceptance of others. She is the person who is happy.

When we become willing to take risks in these ways, "...passion and commitment, love and dedication, self-worth and fulfillment..." will begin to blossom in our lives and true and lasting happiness will fill our souls.

Part Three.
The Finer Details

34　AUSTIN VICKERS

***To become truly happy you must simply do that
which creates happiness.***

The pursuit of happiness is regarded by many as a difficult and complex task. They are right. In fact, the pursuit of happiness is an impossible task for happiness is not something that can be pursued. Happiness, you see, is created. So many of us spend a lifetime going from one circumstance or relationship to the next, continually searching for that which will make us happy. Only we never seem to find it. We may find a circumstance or a relationship that we enjoy for a while, sometimes even years, but eventually the happiness we experience seems to seep away and we are left having to search for a new wellspring from which to draw our happiness.

As simple as it may sound, to become truly happy we do not need to pursue happiness, but rather simply do that which **creates** happiness. Fortunately, life teachers for thousands of years have told us what it is in life that creates true happiness. Moreover, examples abound of individuals who are happy and by and large their recipes for happiness are the same. I have spent a lifetime studying, scrutinizing and analyzing these examples, and numerous philosophies, beliefs, and teachings. I have lived many of the principles contained in such teachings through my own experience. Over the years I have tried to live consciously and in a state of awareness, so that I could draw conclusions from my experience about the effectiveness of these principles. I believe now that I understand how peace of mind and happiness are created.

That does not mean that I live in a state of constant, unending bliss, however. It is one thing to intellectually understand a principle, and quite another to completely live it. But it does mean that I know how to return immediately to a state of happiness when, regardless of the reason, I have become unhappy.

This return is not like simply putting on a cloak of happiness that avoids or represses feelings of unrest or unhappiness. Rather, it is a return to center, to source, to that state of conscious awareness and being that transcends emotional states. It is a return home.

While the understanding of this return process is relatively easy to obtain, and will be laid out in the pages that follow, the implementation of the process is often difficult, especially at first, and it is a lifelong endeavor. The difficulty comes, however, not so much from the process itself, but from our own unwillingness to trust it, or live it. Part of the purpose of our life is to experience unhappiness and unrest, so that through the gifts of these experiences we can learn to appreciate and understand their opposites. Even when we understand how happiness and peace are created, therefore, we still may choose to experience more often than not their opposite states of being. To do so is our choice, our innate right and privilege, and an experience of equal value.

However, it is important to understand how happiness and peace are created, so that our choice of different states of being is a conscious one. One of the most difficult challenges in life is craving the more constant experience of happiness or peace, but not knowing how to create it. To this end, I have funneled what I have learned and experienced about the creation of happiness and peace into a relatively simple principle, or formula. I believe that if you learn to really understand the elements of this formula, and you are willing to trust and follow the process, that happiness and peace will become constant experiences in your life.

The Law of Self Realization

I call this formula the Law of Self Realization. The Law of Self Realization is comprised of several general concepts that prescribe a conscious way of living. If you incorporate these concepts into your life as habits, I believe you will lead a more fulfilled, happy, purposeful, loving life, if that is your choice. Incorporating the ideals of this formula into your life will result in greater happiness, peace and love, and stronger connection to soul, while at the same time preserving the individuality of your purpose and existence.

The Law of Self Realization is as follows:

Happiness = Balance − Expectation + Purpose x Love

It is a rather simple formula, loaded with so much truth. True happiness is created or achieved when we balance our lives, we lose expectation in all things, we have a clearly defined purpose and everything we do is with, and centered in, love. Throughout this book I intend to discuss each of these factors in turn, and show how they are interrelated. I do believe that mastery of the principles contained in this formula will result in happiness at will. The principles have been proven time and time again in the lives and examples of successful and happy people all over the world, spanning many different ages.

But don't trust my words alone. Rather, put the formula to the test for yourself. As I discuss these principles and each of their elements, begin to implement them in your own life. Work on them until they become second nature to you. In no time at all you will begin to see a magical transformation in your life. I say magical, but like in all magic tricks, there is a logical explanation for the effect or the transformation and it is deceivingly simple. Yet for many it remains misunderstood or unknown.

I will show you how the magic works, but it is you that must employ the principles in your life. It is you who must do the work if achieving true happiness and redefining yourself is really your objective. And that, believe it or not, is not a given. Many people say they want to be truly happy, truly peaceful, or have true love in their life. Yet, when it comes time to making the sacrifice of certain behaviors or experiences, and going through the anguish of self-discovery and re-creation, many people are unwilling to take on the task. Their attention soon wanes and before long they are on to something else, some other concept or idea that will capture their intellectual interest for a while. They are unwilling to commit to the work that re-creation demands, and thus they never get to experience its fruits. For these, the words of this book will float aimlessly by and will carry no real lasting meaning.

But for those of you who **really** have a desire to change, who are **ready** to make peace, happiness and love constant choices, and who are ready to do what it takes to achieve these qualities of life, the principles contained in this book will drastically change your life. If you are ready, able and willing to implement them in your life, and are willing to sacrifice the drama associated with their opposite experiences, then you will find within yourself an endless supply of the love, peace and happiness that you seek. That much I can promise.

Balance

To be happy, you must be balanced. To be balanced, body, mind and spirit must be carefully nurtured.

To be truly happy, the first thing you must do is put balance into your life. Whenever we work too much, play too much, give too much, or do anything too much, we put our lives out of balance. Likewise, whenever we do not play enough, or work enough, or invest enough in ourselves, etc., we put our lives out of balance. The lack of balance in our lives leads to frustration, anger, depression, and stress, and unhappiness results. When we focus on maintaining balance, however, we become stronger. Ultimately, we form a base that allows us to focus on other ideals like purpose and love.

There is an inherent beauty in that which is balanced. The wings of a soaring eagle flying through the air, or the bow of a tall sailing ship cutting through the crusted surface of a choppy sea bring to mind the inherent beauty associated with things that are balanced. When a person is balanced, they too are beautiful and grand and their beauty is apparent to all. Balanced individuals display confidence, security, intelligence, patience, and a host of other attributes that result from this state of being. Balanced individuals starkly contrast against those who are imbalanced – who work too much, are too selfish, or those who do not carefully nurture mind, body and spirit. Imbalanced individuals often appear insecure, impatient, egotistical, unstable, and always searching for that which they cannot find.

The importance of balance in our lives can be compared to a three-legged stool. All three legs of the stool are necessary to make it stable and balanced. Take away or shorten one of the legs, and the stool will tip over and become unstable. Likewise, too much length in one of the stool legs, and the stool will be equally unbalanced. In life, we are like the stool and the three legs represent body, mind and spirit. All three of these legs of life are necessary to make us stable and balanced.

Have you ever tried to sit on a three-legged stool that was missing one leg? All of your energy is spent trying to maintain balance and not fall over. You cannot relax. But upon a balanced stool, one can relax, read, work, or use it as a tool to do other things. Likewise in life, when we are not balanced and have not focused enough attention on one of our three legs (mind, body or spirit), all of our energy and focus is spent trying to maintain a balance and not fall.

By now, many people have heard of the body-mind-spirit relationship. This relationship, and the importance of each of its elements, has been the subject of study and discourse by great thinkers for thousands of years. To achieve proper balance in our lives, we cannot neglect our mind, body, or spirit. Like the three-legged stool, not enough focus on any one of the three elements, or too much emphasis on any one or two of the rudiments of this relationship, and our lives will become unbalanced and unhealthy.

In such a state, it becomes difficult to stand upon the stool and reach for loftier heights.

We must care for our physical bodies like we care for our houses, our gardens and our cars. We need to make time in our lives to focus on our minds, stimulating it with nourishing and positive input. And last, but certainly not least, we cannot neglect our spirit - we must notice and nourish it. The element of spirit (or soul) is often neglected, but it requires exercise as much as our bodies and minds. We should feed our souls and make spiritual nourishment a priority in our lives.

Balance in our lives is not a function of genetics or good fortune. It is a carefully and purposefully created habit. Effort should be given each day to work on our mind, body and spirit until doing so becomes second nature to us. Having a sturdy, balanced foundation upon which to center our lives allows us to channel the energy and focus, that was previously spent trying not to fall, toward other more productive and enriching facets of our lives. In other words, having a life of balance means having a life that is not just trying to survive, but having one that is able to thrive.

Body

The body is the vehicle through which the mind and spirit find expression. It is through the body, that the mind and spirit gain a greater appreciation for what they are. Thus, it is the first subject of our discussion on balance.

1.

A healthy body is the surgical tool through which the mind and spirit operate.

It is amazing today to observe the advances of modern medicine. Procedures like heart transplants, complete blood transfusions, removal of tumors and cancers, and artificial limb replacements are almost commonplace, with little fanfare or attention. Advances in technology have fostered many of these "miracles of medicine," as they permit doctors to perform the kinds of operations that just years ago would have been impossible. Devices that allow doctors to see inside of the body and conduct microscopic maneuvers give people requiring such surgeries new hope. In sum, the tools of modern medicine have made surgical doctors more effective than ever.

The human body is the tool by which the mind and spirit operate. If the body is not functioning properly, the mind and spirit can be negatively affected. Conversely, when the body is operating at its peak, the mind is alert and sensations of spirit are much more easily experienced.

Anyone who has had a truly spiritual experience in their life can attest to the physical sensations they had during the experience. The moment becomes almost surreal as the body and mind become engrossed with the spiritual fire that comes from within. The ability to put one's self in a spiritual frame of mind, however, is often dependent on one's ability to tune the body to the experience. This is why meditation or prayer is such an integral part of most spiritual experiences.

The mind cannot function very well if the body is not healthy. Our ability to think, reason, create, etc., is greatly diminished when the attention and focus of our minds is directed to a health problem. People rarely feel like painting when they are suffering from a severe headache or stomach pain. When we are feeling well, however, the body becomes the perfect instrument for allowing the mind and spirit to focus on its tasks, and for experiencing the almost magical effects that come from a creative mind and a free spirit.

We all know how easy it is to take for granted the healthy functioning of the body. As long as we are feeling fine and our attention is elsewhere, we take little notice of the thousands of bodily processes that are working to keep us in a healthy state. However, the moment the body starts to dysfunction, all of our awareness becomes focused on the body and its problems. We become acutely aware of our hurts and our pains. When we ache or are sick it is difficult to focus mentally and is equally difficult to maintain a presence in any spiritual realm. That is because, as the writer and doctor Benjamin Shield once stated, "our body is our most sacred resource available to experience the soul." When this resource is not operating at its fullest potential, the "experience of the soul" is diminished.

Having a healthy body allows us to pursue all other tasks, mental or spiritual, with enthusiasm, vigor, focus, and energy. Without a healthy body, most of our efforts become burdened with the weight and distraction of bodily dysfunction. Care of the body is, therefore, one of our first most important tasks in achieving balance in our lives.

George Santayan once said: "The body is a tabernacle in which the transmissible human spirit is carried for a while, a shell for the immortal seed that dwells in it and has created it." Similarly, Deepak Chopra has noted: "The spirit is nonlocal, but it leaves behind a fingerprint which we call the body. The body is like a young infant and when it is ignored it cries out demanding our attention. The more the body needs our attention, the louder it cries. The trick to preventing the body from having to scream for our attention, like the trick to preventing an infant from screaming for attention, is to pay preventative doses of attention to it before its needs grow too great. The thunder is then taken away before it has any opportunity to cause damage."

To keep our bodies operating at a level where our mind can function efficiently and effectively, and our awareness is free to focus on spirit, we must take care of it. We must nourish it, care for it, and love it. We do this by treating our bodies as if they were a garden.

2.

Fruits of mind and flowers of spirit only flourish in healthy gardens.

Anyone who has ever grown a garden knows that it requires a lot of love, time and attention. The soil must be enriched, seeds must be planted, and water and sunshine must be given in abundance. Weeds, bugs and other animals that can destroy a garden must be kept out. Even when all of these things are done, the garden does not necessarily flourish. It seems that nature must also give her blessing before the fruits and flowers can blossom.

A significant amount of time and attention goes into making

a great garden. Often the rewards of hard work are not seen immediately, but only manifest once the garden is grown; when the flowers bloom, the vegetables mature, and the fruits ripen. And, while the absence of work in a garden on any given day does not usually create a problem, days of absence quickly turn into neglect. Neglecting a garden inevitably results in weeds and rodents entering it, and soon the garden is decayed or destroyed.

The body is like a garden. It, too, requires careful daily attention. The time and effort you spend today on improving your body does not always display itself immediately – rather it manifests in the future. Like the garden, neglect of the body for a short time does not create a problem. But again, habits form easily. One day easily turns into two, and two into a week, and before we know it we have neglected our bodies. Over time this neglect results in premature decay and ultimately destruction if we allow it to advance enough.

Focusing on the body and doing those things that allow it to thrive in the long term are usually not immediately sensed by the body. Few report feeling fantastic after one day of exercise, eating right, or taking a vitamin supplement. However, almost everyone who exercises, who eats right, and supplements their nutrition over the long term reports feelings of well-being and euphoria and usually maintains a healthy, thriving body.

Investment in the body is like the long-term investment in a garden. You should not expect immediate gratification, but rather should understand that your efforts will pay off later. Nourishing the garden of your body today will produce a healthier body tomorrow: one that is more resistant to disease, one that is stronger and fitter, and one that is more able to facilitate tomorrow the crucial work of the mind and spirit.

Many books have been written on the essentials for keeping the body healthy, but in reality, the essence of the best of these books is what you already know to be true. While the media is always touting the latest and greatest fitness craze or radical new diet, the truth of the matter is that the best things for your body are simply the fundamentals: plenty of fresh air; adequate rest; healthy, living foods; fresh water; daily exercise; and attention to balanced nutrition. That's it, no fad diets, no weird machines to work miracles, and no grueling daily routines that would make slave masters proud.

To help you remember these fundamentals, think of the word GARDEN. Each of the letters of the word GARDEN represents one element that is essential for your GARDEN, or your body, to be healthy. The first element is represented by the letter G, which stands for Gardener. No one can have a healthy garden without someone to weed it, feed it, and take care of it. This is the role of the gardener.

3.

A gardener is a garden's way of taking care of itself.

When asked to describe what a physicist was, the famous physicist Neils Bohr once replied: "A physicist is just an atom's way of looking at itself." This answer, while considered by many to be simply a joke, actually carried much more meaning than many people understood. In addition to being witty, his answer conveyed a message that a good scientist or physicist is creative in his approach to solving problems. A good scientist will consider many different perspectives when trying to resolve an issue, including turning things upside-down to find an answer.

Through his response Neils Bohr unveiled the earmark of any successful thinker: to find the truth you must consider different perspectives and be willing to look at things from the opposite of your normal perspective. One can look at the relationship between mind and body the same way. Was the mind created so the body would have a way of expressing itself and viewing itself, or was the body created so the mind could find physical expression? The answer to this question could fill volumes. The point for this discussion, however, is that when focusing on the care of the body, you cannot look at the body by itself. You must also consider the mind, for the mind is the vehicle through which the body looks at itself and improves itself. The two work hand in hand for personal growth.

Thus, if you think of your body as a GARDEN, think of your mind as the gardener. Your mind is what is responsible for the care of the body, for exerting the will, discipline, and stimulation necessary for the body to care for itself. Without the gardener, the garden can grow out of control and become choked with weeds, burrs and bristles. Likewise, without the mental exertion of will and discipline, the body can destroy itself.

The mind plays an important role in the improvement of the body. For example, science over the last decade has unearthed an enormous amount of evidence that proves that visualization has positive effects on the body. This is true, for example, in the conditioning of athletes. In one study it was shown that basketball players who visualized making free throws each day improved in their free-throw shooting capabilities almost as much as those that actually shot free throws every day.

To make physical changes in our bodies, we need to begin to lose the negative perceptions we have of ourselves and begin to see ourselves in a whole new way. Beginning today, you should begin to think of yourself as that which you wish to become. Thoughts always precede action and without imagining positive changes in yourself, such changes become more difficult to occur. Thus, if you view the state of your physical health in a negative way, i.e., that you are sick all of the time, or you are too fat or too skinny, you must begin to alter your perceptions. Positive changes breed confidence and confidence breeds more positive changes. These changes begin with your own mental perceptions. Change them for the better and you will begin to manifest positive changes in your physical being.

Attitude plays a significant role in the maintenance of our bodies. We can always find weakness in ourselves. But if we are fair, we can always find strengths as well. The choice is yours as to where you will focus your attention. But remember that a change in your attitude will alter your experience. If I give you a rose, you not only receive its precious petals, but you also receive its thorns. If your attention is given to the thorns, then the gift may become an experience of pain. However, if your attention is given to the petals, then the gift will become an experience of beauty. By refocusing your attention on the positive aspects of your body, you will change your physical experience from one of pain to one of beauty.

Another tool you can use to tend to your garden, or your body, is the exertion of will and discipline to change bad habits. You know what your bad habits are – whether you smoke, overeat, drink too much, or deprive your body of exercise or rest. These habits did not appear spontaneously or innately, rather they were developed by your habitual action or inaction. Thus, you can use action or inaction to "undo" any negative habits you may have developed.

One of the easiest ways to change a habit, according to the Duke University Medical Center, is to recognize and define the steps leading to the performance of the habit, and then introduce a step in the process prior to performance of the habit to remind yourself not to go through with it. This step should also help you to establish a newer, healthier habit.

For example, let's assume that you are in the habit of eating potato chips every night while watching your favorite television show. You notice that just before you watch a program, you go into the kitchen, pour yourself a drink, and then you go to the cupboard for a bag of chips to eat during the program. Since these are the steps you take to accomplish your habit, you need to introduce a new step in the process to remind yourself that you should not eat potato chips every night. So, for example, you might try putting a sign in your cupboard where you normally put the potato chips that says: "Chips are fattening – eat an apple." Or you might include a note in your shopping list reminding you not to buy any chips for the same reason and to replace it with a healthier food. Whatever your bad habit may be, chances are you follow a process before you engage in it. You can alter this process to help you avoid the bad habit.

The most important thing you can do to improve your physical well-being is to become aware of that which deprives you of well-being. That may sound awfully simple, but there is an amazing amount of people who do not spend the time thinking about the cause of their physical problems. To change bad habits, to improve the quality of your garden or your body, you must identify that which detracts from its quality. Then use this awareness to motivate yourself to change, to try new patterns of behavior that enhance, rather than detract, from your physical state of well-being.

Do not underestimate the role of your mind, the gardener, in the care of your bodily garden. As you will read later in the section on the mind, everything becomes possible if you set your mind to it. You are not stuck with any "bad habits." All habits can be recreated into behaviors that contribute to the health and well-being of your body. It simply requires that your gardener (your mind) be willing to implement positive changes to undo those bad habits.

4.

***Air is the lifeblood of our bodily existence,
without which the body cannot survive.***

The "A" in GARDEN, and the next element that we must insist be a part of our lives if we want to have a healthy body, stands for air. Everyone needs clean fresh air. Air is the lifeblood of our existence and without it we cannot survive. The average human being will die within minutes of oxygen deprivation. Air is truly the life force that flows within us and through us. Air constantly feeds our lungs, our cells, and our blood. The oxygen that comes from air is utilized by every part of our body.

The rich oxygen that we need to breathe is produced by plants and trees. The more we remove and destroy plants and trees from our earth, the more we destroy our ability to have and use good, clean air. The more we destroy our access to good, clean air, the more we destroy our life force.

The air we breathe is also one vehicle by which nature causes energy to circulate upon the earth. The air we breathe today carries the energy once utilized by our ancestors. That energy flows to and from people around the world, and will be utilized by our children's children. The more we pollute this air, the more we cause it to become a vehicle of sickness rather than a vehicle of life.

The ill effects on the body that come from smoking, pollution and other toxins in the air are now well documented. Yet, we see these abusive practices continuing. Our society exists on a "live for the moment" philosophy that will ultimately do exactly that: allow us to just "live for the moment." As long as we continue to destroy trees and vegetation and abuse the air we breathe, we won't have to worry too much about our future – for ultimately there will not be one.

Although we have grown accustomed to living in cities, driving cars, living and working in air-conditioned houses and offices, etc., we ought to recognize that these habits starve our bodies of much needed fresh air. Fresh air deprivation is not something that in one day will harm our bodily gardens. But over time it will cause our fruits and flowers to stop growing. Take the time each day to find and fill your lungs with good, clean fresh air. If you can live outside of a city, closer to nature, do so. If you cannot, fill your living environment with as many plants and trees as you can. Remember that filling your lungs with clean, fresh air is an investment in the future of your garden.

You should also spend time each day focusing on your breathing, moving it from short, shallow breaths, to long, deep breaths that expand and fill your lungs. Breathing properly is an important exercise and one that indicates the emotional state of our being. When we breathe in rapid, shallow, short breaths, it is an indication that we are feeling stressed, tense and anxious. When we breathe in slow, deep, long breaths, it is evidence of a state of relaxation and tranquility. Thus, the state of our being affects our rate of breathing.

But the opposite is also true. The way we breathe can also help create the state of our being. That is why all meditation begins with a focus on the state of breathing. Taking long, slow, deep breaths contributes to a mental and spiritual state of awareness and perception. But we should not be concerned with our breathing only during meditation. We can benefit from a focus on breathing properly throughout the day. Consequently, become aware of the state of your breathing at all times. Slow your breathing down and practice taking long, deep breaths that fill your lungs completely. This practice will help create a body that easily facilitates the workings of mind and spirit.

5.

Peace of mind and body is the state in which all growth occurs.

The R in our bodily GARDEN stands for rest. A healthy garden needs time when it is not being fed, cultivated, weeded or watered. Once it has been properly cared for, a garden needs time to be left alone, so that it can actually grow. It is during this "rest time" that a garden will grow the most: when it is simply ***being***.

Our bodies are the same way. We feed them, work them, exercise them and entertain them. But often we do not sufficiently rest them. Your body is set up on natural rhythms that are cyclical in nature. When your body is out of rhythm, it will also be out of balance. Our sleep patterns are part of our bodily rhythms, and thus it is important that you establish a good pattern that allows you enough sleep on a daily basis.

When the body gets sick, the first thing it does is demand rest. The energy levels of the body go down, fatigue sets in quickly, and sleep becomes an imperative. This process occurs because it is during this rest time that the body heals itself. While resting, the body can concentrate on growth and refueling for future activity.

Nowadays, it is not uncommon for many people in the traditional work environment to complain of chronic fatigue, or always being tired. Yet many of these same individuals work all day, party all night, and do not listen to their bodies when they become tired and ask for rest. Then, they wonder why they get sick. The sickness is merely the body's way of being heard in its need for rest.

We must listen more to what our bodies tell us. If your body is constantly tired, then it means it needs more rest. It may need that rest because there is a problem. You should try to determine if you have a problem if you think you are tired more than what is normal for you. But do not ignore the body's request: give your body the rest that it is asking for at the same time that you try to discover the problem.

There is no set amount of time each day that you should sleep or rest. While many people think eight hours is the right amount of time, only you can decide what is right for you. If you sleep eight hours and you still feel tired, you obviously need more sleep or your body is trying to tell you something else.

Listen to your body and trust that it will dictate that which you really need. In this way, you honor your body by recognizing and appreciating its instructions. When you vindicate the body's messages to you, you open the way for more insight. When you block or ignore the body's messages, you close the door for such insights.

While you may believe that your feelings of fatigue are possibly due to a physical health problem or are just your body's way of trying to get you a couple of extra hours of sleep on a weekend to "catch up," in fact your body may be telling you much more. People who listen to their hearts and follow their intuitions and passions for the first time often report feeling massive amounts of new energy. Where they historically felt tired while working in mundane jobs that did not align with what their hearts and spirits were telling them they should do, once they begin to follow their hearts and spirits, their energy returns and the fatigue passes.

We see evidence of this phenomenon all the time. How often do we feel tired and fatigued and have a hard time getting up in the morning before work, but when it comes to the weekend and we have the opportunity to pursue our passions, we spring right out of bed with no trouble at all? The difference between the two is a message from our souls.

The body not only grows tired of physical activity, but also tires of pursuing that which does not satisfy the soul.

We have spiritual obligations to ourselves to pursue the dreams and desires of our hearts, and when we do so, the body responds positively. When we are pursuing passions and "soul work," we no longer need the amount of rest that our bodies demand while doing other things that do not feed our souls or advance our purpose in life. We can get up early in the morning, go to bed later at night, and still feel a wellspring of energy inside.

When we are pursuing that which does not advance our purpose of being, however, we feel fatigued, we lack energy, and we become tired despite the amount of rest we receive. Our zest and enthusiasm for life becomes severely diminished. If we do not heed the signs of our body to "rest" from that which leaves us unfulfilled, in time our bodies will break down and our gardens will become overgrown with weeds, unable to produce sweet fruits and fresh flowers.

The only escape from this result is to heed the signs from our bodies, to get more rest, and to abandon those life activities that sap our energy and our passion. Begin to spend more time fulfilling your passions and your life's purpose, and your energy and life force will return. If you had enough money and would do for free what you are doing with your work today, there is a good chance you are following your passion. If there is no chance you would do for free what you are doing today, then chances are you are selling yourself short. Chances are you are ignoring what your heart and spirit are telling you should be done. Chances are you are also suffering from excessive fatigue, or you will be.

Do that which your spirit tells you to do today. Find your passions and take the risks necessary to pursue them. Let your self succumb to spirit and begin a new adventure that follows the promptings of your heart and soul. When you do, you will find renewed energy, renewed vitality, and a driving passion that will feed your body and allow your mind and spirit to grow. Your body will truly become a sharp, surgical instrument that allows your mind and spirit to operate fully.

6.

> *"Our bodies are . . . communities in relationship with the earth. Our bodily fluids carry the same chemicals as the primeval seas . . . Our bones contain the sugar that once flowed in the sap of non-fossilized trees. The nitrogen which binds our bones together is the same as that which binds nitrates to the soil."*
> — James Nelson

No garden can thrive and grow without proper nourishment. Without receiving nutrients and minerals from the soil, without sunshine, and without water, plants and flowers would wither and die. Likewise, no body can be physically strong in the long run without receiving the appropriate amount of nourishment. Thus, the D in our bodily GARDEN stands for the next important contribution we must give to the body: diet.

By diet I do not mean "going on a diet" or dieting. In fact, I mean the exact opposite of dietary restriction. By diet, I mean what it is that we feed our bodies. Like most areas of physical health, a lot has been written concerning the nutritional needs of the human body. These needs are met most simply by whatever it is we decide to put in our mouths. And of course, depending upon what choices we make to feed ourselves, sometimes our dietary needs are met and sometimes they are not.

It is not my intention to go into great detail regarding the specific kinds of foods and drinks that are healthy for the body and those that are not. Enough has been written on this subject that it is relatively easy to find good books dedicated to the specifics of human nutrition. It is my intent, however, to cover a few simple rules or philosophies of nutrition that, if followed, will help your body maintain itself at maximum efficiency and be more capable of enabling your mind and spirit to operate.

One adage worth remembering is: if you want life, eat live foods. If you want death, eat dead foods. Live foods of course mean anything that grows. You cannot eat too much fruit, vegetables, grains, nuts, etc. Foods that are derived from living plants, vegetables, trees, etc., can and should be eaten in abundance in their natural form.

The goodness that exists in a potato, for example, can bring good health to anyone who eats it. However, think what the average person does to this vegetable. First we peel it, stripping it of the nutrients and minerals contained in its skin. Then we boil it for some time, making sure that none of its nutrients survive. Then we beat what is left of it until it no longer even resembles a potato. Next, we add massive amounts of butter, milk and salt to make it taste better! What is left can hardly be called a potato.

The same is true for many of the vegetables we eat, or the grains we process into breads, cereals, etc. The processing of these wholesome foods strips them of the richness of the minerals, vitamins and nutrients naturally found within them. The best way to eat anything that grows is in its natural state. If you must cook anything at all to soften texture, try steaming things. Steaming at least helps preserve some of their natural goodness.

You should also try to avoid eating dead foods. A good rule of thumb to follow here is any food that is prepared in such a way that if you were treated in the same way it would kill you, is probably a dead food and should be avoided. So, for example, anything that is killed in order to be eaten, or is boiled, fried, baked, micro-waved past the point of heating, etc., could be considered a "dead food" and will not bring to your body the same level of "wholeness" that is available through raw foods. While such foods are often pleasant to the taste, they can be killers over the long term as they are usually loaded with salt and fat.

Many people have difficulty keeping to a natural diet because they do not believe such foods "taste good" and they prefer the taste of junk foods. Food companies spend millions of dollars each year, advertising on television, in magazines and on the radio to help create positive mental associations with the food products they sell. As a result, we see family being associated with hamburgers and fries, and attractive women being associated with alcohol and tobacco, etc. These associations and the eating habits we have brought from childhood form the basis for our "tastes" and "preferences." However, our tastes and preferences are not fixed. They, too, can be altered.

When most people see a fatty food like a hamburger, they think about how good that food would taste if they were to eat it. Often these foods remind people of summer barbecues, or outings with friends and families, which are all positive associations. This sort of positive association will do nothing but encourage you to eat fatty, unhealthy foods. This is exactly what the food companies that sell these products want you to think and feel, that is why they spend so much money advertising their products in this way.

To lose this desire to consume such foods, you must begin to attach to them negative associations. For example, if every time you saw a hamburger that was tempting to eat, you thought of those television images you may have seen involving a liposuction procedure, where transparent needles and tubes are stuck in a person and large amounts of slimy, coagulated fat are extracted from their body parts, and you associated the fat of the hamburger with the fat coming out of the body, over time you would create a negative association with the hamburger and you would lose your taste or preference for it.

Vegetarians often report that while they once may have

loved fatty and fried foods, after eliminating them from their diet and "learning" to eat natural foods, they now become repulsed by the thought of eating meats and fatty foods. When they think of foods like hamburgers and hotdogs, they are reminded of all of the fat, chemicals and steroids that are used to produce such foods. Learning to create negative associations with unhealthy foods, and positive associations with healthy foods, will "alter" your taste preferences, and lead you to a more nutritious, healthy diet.

Another good rule of thumb to follow is to choose natural over synthetic whenever possible. While science continues to amaze us with what they have discovered and what they can duplicate, they still have not learned to create life from nothing, like Mother Nature can do. While they may be able to duplicate the chemical formulation of a particular nutrient, etc., what they cannot duplicate is the "life force" or "energy" that exists beyond the simple chemical formulation. Only nature can do this. Consequently, if you have the choice between a natural product and a synthetic one, choose the natural one. The sacrifice you may have to pay in terms of convenience or price will be more than worth the healthy state your body will assume once you choose "living things" with which to nourish it.

Other than food, the other important element of diet is water. We know that our bodies are more water than anything else. It is also obvious that the purer the water we put into our bodies, the purer will be the water that exists in our bodies. Focus everyday on putting into your body at least 8 glasses of pure, natural water. As water is the most prevalent substance in your body, you must keep your "pool of water" as clean and fresh as possible. Drinking fresh clean water each day in abundance will allow you to accomplish this goal. There is no replacement for water in terms of your health and it is important that water forms an instrumental part of your daily liquid routine.

For variation, fruit and vegetable juices should make up the balance of your liquid investment. Again, strive here for the most natural approach, choosing unpasteurized or unprocessed juices, as they will bring your body the most nourishment. Avoid liquids that are addictive or contain chemicals. This will include, of course, the majority of what most people drink – sodas, coffee, tea, and alcohol. These products are loaded with chemicals and sugar and in many cases actually dehydrate you (remove water from your body) rather than hydrate you (put water into your body). Fill your body with clean, refreshing water and learn to develop a taste preference for water.

No discussion of diet and nutrition would be complete without raising the issue of vitamin and mineral supplementation. While historically there has been much debate in the medical community over the issue of supplementation, recent years have seen a flood of research showing the benefits of various vitamin and mineral supplements. While theoretically, we should be able to eat enough raw foods in sufficient variety to provide our bodies with all of its vitamin and mineral needs, the reality of modern eating habits is that we do not get enough vitamins and minerals from the food we eat. Consequently, as an insurance policy to our eating habits, taking a multi-mineral, multi-vitamin supplement ensures that we meet most of our daily vitamin and mineral needs.

While most people are aware of the body's need for vitamins, many are unaware of the importance of minerals. The body is comprised of at least 31 known chemical elements, of which 24 are considered to be essential for sustaining life. These essential elements are combined in thousands of different ways to form the various life supporting structures that exist within your body.

The most abundant nonmetal, chemical element in the body is oxygen, which amounts to 65% of a person's weight. Thus, you can see the need for good, clean air. Three other nonmetal elements constitute 31% of the body's mass: carbon 18%; hydrogen 10%; and nitrogen 3%. The remaining 4% is composed of a group of 22 metallic elements called minerals. Although the total quantity of these minerals in the body is relatively small, each of them is vital for proper cell functioning, and the absence of any of them over the long term can cause serious health problems. Consequently, vitamin/mineral supplementation reduces the risk that any of these mineral elements will be lacking in the body.

Beyond general supplementation, the use of herbs and plants should be considered as often as possible, especially when you are sick. Of course, you should find a natural minded physician with whom you can discuss objectively the natural remedies you may wish to use to heal your body. A good, objective, natural minded physician can provide you with the right balance of advice as to when herbs or natural therapy will suffice for your treatment, or when more serious medical treatment may be necessary.

In sum, feed your body with live foods, replenish it with plenty of fresh clean water, supplement it with vitamins and minerals, and use plants and herbs liberally. If you follow these simple rules, your garden will flourish.

7.

An active body facilitates an active mind and spirit.

Fruits, vegetables, or flowers do not grow very well in a garden that is not properly pruned, cultivated, or weeded. These activities require time and effort. When we spend time and effort in a garden doing these things, the results are spectacular: fruits become sweeter to the taste, vegetables appear richer in flavor and appearance, and flowers overwhelm us with their beauty.

Likewise, you should spend time cultivating your bodily garden. You do this by exercising. Consequently, the E in our GARDEN metaphor stands for exercise.

There are plenty of reasons to exercise your body, not the least of which is your simple, physical health. In a medical study conducted by the Stanford University School of Medicine on 17,000 Harvard alumni, it was found that those who burned more than 2,000 calories a week exercising had a death rate from all causes that was 28 percent lower than those who exercised less or not at all. In other words, more than one out of four people who begin to implement an exercise regimen will have a longer life as a result of that exercise. This statistic does not even take into account the length or quality of life that is enhanced significantly because of exercise.

Exercising, according to most medical experts, has been proven to do the following: lower your risk of heart disease; lower your risk of several forms of cancer; lower your stress level; improve your blood sugar level; improve your lung capacity and functioning; improve your cardiovascular function; increase your muscle strength; lower your cholesterol level; increase your flexibility; improve your balance; improve your sleep patterns; decrease your depression and fatigue; improve your ability to think and remember; and improve your physical appearance. In sum, exercise has enormous benefits to the body and significantly improves its ability to function. Not to mention that a body that functions properly creates room for an active mind and spirit.

The worst thing people do when they begin an exercise program is to incorporate activities into their routine that they do not enjoy. They also usually begin so dramatically and intensely, that a few days later their body feels worse than it did before they started. Then they lose the motivation to continue. To avoid this kind of result you should plan an exercise routine made up of several different activities that you enjoy.

Your body actually responds better to exercise when the activities you engage in are constantly changing. This prevents your muscles from acting out of habit, as they begin to do when your exercise routine becomes too repetitious. To increase muscular fitness, burn fat, or improve the level of energy exerted in exercise, it is more important to make your muscles act as a result of inertia or directed energy, rather than from repeated motion. Engaging in different kinds of exercise helps you achieve this objective, as well as helping to keep you from losing interest in exercise or getting bored.

There are literally thousands of activities you can engage that benefit your body. Activities such as jogging, running, walking, cycling, swimming, skiing, sports, etc., are but a few suggestions of things you can do. As long as you enjoy the activity and it makes your heart pump a little quicker, chances are it will be good for you. At a minimum, however, you should try to do at least 20 – 30 minutes of exercise a day, at least five days a week.

Before you get started on an exercise routine there are few things you should do. Consult your doctor and make sure that the exercises you choose are in accordance with your health history and health status. For example, bungee jumping is probably not a good start for someone with a history of heart problems. Also, try to choose activities that are aerobic in nature, or that consist of moderate, rhythmic and continuous movements of your large muscle groups. Make sure that you properly stretch and warm up before you begin your exercises. Not only will stretching, in and of itself, provide you with physical benefits, but it can prevent injuries from occurring during the performance of the activity.

Set realistic goals for yourself with respect to exercise. Do not overdo it or believe that you must engage in masochistic behavior or practices to benefit from the activity. Believe it or not, your body benefits greatly from many physical activities that are also fun. Finally, try to build some movement into every part of your life. While technology constantly creates ways for you to reduce your energy output through the invention of automatic everythings, abandon some of these conveniences and take the time to introduce more physical exertion into your life. Rediscover what it is like to take the stairs instead of the elevator; cut your own lawn and garden; do the dishes instead of using a dishwasher; or walk somewhere instead of taking your car. Make your exercise routine varied and fun and it will not be long until exercise becomes a part of your life that figuratively, and literally, you cannot live without.

As you begin to incorporate exercising into your life, you will feel better, look better, and most importantly your body will actually *be* better. As this transformation takes place, your body will allow your mind to operate more efficiently and effectively, and your body and mind will be a vessel where spirit is warmly welcomed.

The other benefit that exercise will bring you is more exposure to nature, as many of the activities you may choose will be associated with the outdoors. This brings us to the last letter of our GARDEN metaphor, the letter N, which stands for nature. Nature brings many benefits to the body, mind and spirit.

8.

> *"Nature is the living, visible garment of God."*
> *- Goethe*

All around us we are blessed with the results of divine creation, for nature and everything in it clearly is the greatest evidence existing to prove the reality of God. We take nature for granted: we poison her lakes, rivers and oceans; we fill her lands with poisons and toxins; and we pollute her air with chemicals, smog and pollution. And, yet, nature still shares her beauty and provides the basis on which we exist.

Anyone who has taken the time to hike up a rugged mountain, swim in a mountain lake or river, or simply enjoy the beauty and color of wild flowers, will find it difficult to ignore the hand of divine creation in nature. For all of mankind's technical achievements, he still cannot duplicate the awe-inspiring scenery that nature provides.

You cannot spend too much time with nature. Whether it is time spent in your garden, or an adventure planned in the wild, **being** in nature allows nature to contribute to your state of being. In nature our lungs are filled with clean, fresh air; our mouths taste the rich flavor of pure water; our eyes behold the wondrous beauty of mountains, trees, animals and cloud formations; our nostrils sense the distinct odors of plants, trees and earth; and our ears delight to the songs of life that surround us. All of our senses become engaged in nature, and our souls are nourished, uplifted and rewarded.

Whenever we spend time in nature we become reminded of its value and we often wish we had more time to spend there. That is because nature is real. When we escape to nature we become relaxed and appreciative of the beauty around us. We become less stressed and we work at a more natural pace. In essence, when we engross ourselves in nature, we become synchronized to the natural rhythms of life and our bodies respond positively. All living things have vibration and energy and between living things this energy and life is shared. Indeed it is how we communicate at the level of spirit. In nature we become energized, active and alert because we absorb and share so much of the energy and life that exists there.

Our minds and spirits also respond positively to nature. In nature, our minds become alive, and we become creative, imaginative and playful. Some of the best thinking I have ever done is when I am alone with my thoughts in nature. In nature our spirits also come alive, and we instinctively feel a connection with the life around us. Many magical moments occur in nature, for spirit feels at home there. For many it is also easier to find God there.

Living in cities we lose track of what is natural and real because we are so inundated with what is unreal and unnatural; material images, product advertising, and synthetic everything. When we deprive ourselves of time with nature we become tired, stressed, hurried, overworked, and un-appreciative: we suffer from general malaise. Most people will acknowledge this fact when they become so stressed they admit the need to "get away." Removed from nature we become methodic, dull, unimaginative and preoccupied with "matters that don't."

Tatanga Mani once succinctly stated about nature: "Hills are always more beautiful than stone buildings, you know. Living in the city is an artificial existence. Lots of people hardly ever feel real soil under their feet, see plants grow except in flower pots, or get far enough beyond the street light to catch the enchantment of a night sky studded with stars. When people live far from scenes of the Great Spirit's making, it's easy for them to forget his laws."

When we spend time in nature we cannot help but see and feel the hand of God's creation. With all of its natural splendor nature reminds us of our place - not in dominion over the elements, but rather in coexistence. The energy of the universe that created this planet and every living thing on it is the same that courses through our bodies. This energy, our energy, existed long before our physical manifestation and it will exist long after it.

When we step into and surround ourselves with nature's creations, we merge closely with the energy we equally share. This ultimately means that nature gets to participate in our energy as equally as we get to participate in its. That is why we become energized when we return to nature. That is why we feel more alive, why we sleep better, feel more energetic, become more creative and become better balanced.

The importance of nature to our body, mind and soul is why we must begin to take better care of nature. We happily use nature to satisfy our own needs, but we do not actively work to protect and preserve her for future generations. We cannot do enough to protect our waters, lakes, rivers and oceans, or ensure that our air is clean and our land is not polluted. Be active in causes that strive to protect the sensitive eco-balance of nature. Unfortunately, nature is a resource that once spent cannot be reproduced. Thus, we cannot afford to make any mistakes. We need to act now to preserve what we have.

In sum, we will have a better bodily GARDEN when nature becomes a priority in our lives, as our body, mind and spirit all respond positively to the gracious gift God has given us. Make nature a part of your life. Learn to appreciate and care for her in the same way that she heals you, energizes you, and lovingly cares for your spirit.

9.

Where you find joy and laughter, so too will you find a body that can heal itself.

One of the most remarkable aspects of children is there complete willingness to be happy, to be joyful, and to laugh. Children do not need much reason to be happy, they are content to amuse themselves with whatever they can find that makes them laugh. I have heard many adults comment, when they are viewing the frivolity of children, how easily they are amused. We should all be so easily amused.

Children laugh because they have not yet lost their joy. They are passionate human beings that focus easily on the present moment, and they have not yet developed their "image" enough to allow it to destroy their joy. They have not yet learned to be cynical or judgmental and they have not learned how to hold grudges. And so they don't; they forgive us quickly when we cause them upset and they return to happiness and joy as quickly as we move from one thought to the next.

Somewhere in the process of growing up we lose the wonderful attributes of children. We lose their creativity, interest in life, passion, hope, belief, trust, and so many of their exceptional qualities. Somewhere along the way, as adults, we replace these loving attributes with cynicism, judgment, hardness, and we seem to loose much of our joy. It is almost as if, as grown-ups, we cannot be happy like children because we are **obligated** to be burdened with the "realities" of a more complex life.

But what is more real than the joy, happiness and laughter that children manage to find every day in any circumstance? What is more real than the ability of children to immediately forgive, and return to laughter and joy after experiencing emotional upset or anger? What is more real than the exceptional ability children have to live in the present moment?

We have a lot to learn from children. Perhaps, however, the most important things we can re-learn are their sense of play and their ability to be silly, to laugh out loud, to be happy, to be curious, and to have joy without regard to what others "think." Remember back to the days when you were a child and you allowed yourself to be happy and joyful. Your life was filled with fun. You were creative, hopeful, imaginative, forgiving, and freely loving. You could be upset with someone one minute, and best friends the next. You lived completely in the present, never harboring negative feelings from your past and not worrying too much about your future.

To return to joy and fill your life once again with the amazing quality of childlike delight, you need simply to emulate children. Let go of the concern you have over what other people think. Let go of what is proper to do or behavior you are afraid "does not conform." Watch what children do and allow yourself to be like them.

Learn once again the value of being silly.

One of my favorite experiences I have with my children at the dinner table is taking turns trying to make funny faces that cause each other to laugh. We make the silliest, most bizarre and contorted faces imaginable. When we want to get really serious at making each other laugh, we take turns trying not to smile while the other person does their best to make us smile. I know of no other game that is so much fun to lose.

We do not laugh enough at ourselves. We do not act silly enough. We care too much about what others think is appropriate. We do not smile enough. Smiling, you know, in and of itself, can cause you to be happy. The next time you are feeling sad or depressed, try plastering a smile on your face for a minute or so. It will become real. Smiling is infectious and positively affects everyone around you.

It is now well documented what a positive mental attitude can do for health problems. Every human ailment, from colds to cancer, has been proven to be more easily overcome with a positive mental attitude. Smiling, joking, and laughing put us into a positive frame of mind. Thus, quite literally, joy and laughter can heal us. Smiling, laughter, silliness, and joy can be shared with everyone at no personal cost. In most cases, they are returned in kind and our world naturally becomes a happier place. Without joy and laughter in our lives, our problems begin to overwhelm us. Soon stress and dis-ease enter the picture and it is not long until our bodies begin to suffer and break down. But when we allow joy and laughter to fill our lives and overcome our problems, we allow peace and happiness to enter our lives and the lives of those we touch.

When we can be silly, laugh out loud, smile often, and create joy, we begin to deflate our problems. When we deflate our problems, we heal them. When we heal our problems, we heal ourselves. When we heal ourselves, we heal the world.

10.

Music is the rhythm of spirit.

Since the very beginning of time music has been used by man as a celebration of life. Whether it is the union of two people in marriage, the birth of a child, community, or the mourning of a loved one lost, music has always been our expression of feeling, mood and sentiment. It seems there is a song for every occasion, one for every feeling of the heart. Musical expression has also had a historical evolution that has allowed it to transform itself to accurately portray the feelings and moods of entire generations. Thus, specific types of music have become important earmarks of a generation or culture.

Music forms an integral part of all cultural experience and comes in many different forms. From the didgeridoos of the Aborigines of Australia, to the drums of the native North American Indians, to the wind instruments of Northern Ireland, to the Flamenco guitars of Spain, we have created different instruments to better represent the sounds we hear in our hearts. These sounds, these inner rhythms, when expressed through music, can represent anger, sadness, joy, sexuality, frivolity, or a host of other human feelings. As complex as these emotions can be, so too is the music that represents them.

I think everyone can relate to the experience of hearing a particular song from the past that immediately takes us back to the moments when we first embraced its melody. Such songs flood our minds with the images and feelings that we had at the time. There are still songs that I can hear from my own past that make me immediately laugh or cry, or put me mentally in the arms of a past loved one. In fact, much of this book was written while listening to many of my favorites musicians, like Enya, Jewel, or the Corrs: musicians whose music always help me become more creative and puts me closer to my spirit.

I think most people can relate to the emotions that certain music evokes in each of us. Music can inspire us to think, laugh, cry, reflect, sing, dance, make love, become angry or passive, or feel in a myriad of different ways. These responses to music are feelings that come from our hearts, which is the home of the spirit. Thus, quite literally, music is a human, bodily way of accessing and imitating the sounds of spirit.

By now the positive effects of music in life are well established. Surgeons, for example, often play music in the operating room, not only because of the calming effect that it has on their staff, but also because of the positive effect it has on their patients – even when they are under anesthesia.

Likewise, music has been scientifically proven to enhance linear thinking in children. Scientists have reported that children who are exposed to classical music at an early age develop significantly quicker than other children. Those exposed to music at an early age have, on average, a higher IQ throughout life than those who are not routinely exposed to music.

While at first blush these facts may surprise some people, they actually are quite logical when we better understand what music actually is and how it relates to what we actually are. Music is nothing but a pattern of changing vibrations. The string on the guitar when struck resonates and vibrates to create a particular sound. A piano makes sounds when a soft mallet strikes a piano's strings, causing them to vibrate. These vibrations are then organized into patterns, which become notes and eventually songs. Music is the result. In sum, music is simply a changing pattern of vibrational energy.

So are we.

The energy or vibration of music interacts with our own energy. Depending upon the kind of music we listen to, we either create harmony or disharmony between the energy of the music we are listening to and that which forms our bodies. When the energy of music resonates with the energy within us, harmony is created and positive feelings and emotions result. When the vibration of the music conflicts with our own vibrations, disharmony is created and anxiety and stress can result. That is why, at times, certain forms of music go with certain moods or feelings we are experiencing, or indeed why music can create certain moods or feelings within us.

Whether consciously or subconsciously, music greatly affects us. Certain types of music can have a disorienting and a chaotic effect on our bodily vibrations. Other types of music will have a harmonizing effect on the body, and in fact, can soothe, calm and heal the body.

There is no correct or incorrect type of music. The vibrations within us are as varied as the many types of music, instruments and sounds that exist. The only type of music that is wrong for us is that which creates disharmony. Likewise, the right kind of music for us is that which positively influences our lives. Only you can be the judge of what kind of music inspires you or diminishes your experience.

The point that must be made regarding music, however, is that we should make it an instrumental part (pun intended) of our lives, choosing that which elevates, motivates and inspires us. Pay attention to the words of music and choose to listen to songs whose choruses uplift and nourish your soul. Expose your children to music and teach them an appreciation and a love for uplifting sounds. Teach them, and learn yourself, how to play and extract from instruments their soul-feeding melodies.

When we create music, we create energy and this energy radiates from us like a ripple in a pond. This energy can indeed motivate and inspire, make us laugh or cry, and positively affect our lives and the lives of others. Music is one of the body's tools for healing and nurturing itself and we can use music to heal and nourish others as well. Music is also another way to passionately express our love for others.

In sum, music is our body's way of hearing what spirit is.

11.

The glory of the body is manifested through its senses.

We have spent a fair amount of time talking about the proper care and nourishment of the body. When we understand the purpose of the body and we take proper care of it, we become free to experience its glory. The glory of the body is manifested through its senses.

Most of us take for granted the physical experience that is brought to our minds and souls by the body. For those of us lucky enough to have all of our senses intact, we often overlook the fact that we **can** see, **can** hear, **can** smell, **can** taste, and **can** touch. We tend to focus only on the information provided to us by these senses. Or we employ these senses almost automatically, never attaching our awareness to their processes to more fully engage them.

True appreciation starts first with awareness. There is great physical, mental and spiritual value in becoming more aware of our senses and focusing our attention on them. As we begin to utilize our senses consciously, rather than unconsciously, life becomes filled with richer detail, we become more present moment focused, and our mental and spiritual abilities are enhanced as our appreciation grows.

Everyone has heard stories of someone who, having lost one of their senses because of injury or accident, develops uncanny abilities with one of their remaining senses. Most common are stories of people who develop incredible hearing abilities after becoming blind. Some, for example, become able to distinguish individuals by the sound of their breathing while others see a substantial increase in their tonal ranges, becoming able to discern and hear sounds that were once inaudible to their ears.

What is important to learn from such examples is the cause of these significantly improved senses. Obviously, the basic physical structure of their sensory organs does not change. What changes is simply their awareness and appreciation. Having reduced five senses down to four, or four senses down to three, their awareness and focus heightens on their remaining senses. This awareness and focus causes those senses to dramatically improve. They also more fully appreciate their senses that remain intact.

What this should mean to us is that we do not have to lose one of our senses to fully develop the others. By simply raising the level of our awareness and appreciation for our sight, hearing, our smell, our taste or our touch, we can dramatically improve their functioning.

Begin, consciously, each day to stop and consider each of your senses and the experiences they are bringing you. What beautiful things can you see with your eyes? Try to find something. Can you hear someone laughing? Find a flower to indulge your sense of smell. Challenge yourself to taste something you have not experienced before. And finally, find someone in your life, anyone, and touch them - give them a huge hug.

We simply do not hug enough. We have lost the value of touch. When someone we do not know tries to share a hug with us, we usually respond awkwardly or timidly. We prefer to keep people at arm's length, rather than wrap our arms around them. Many families even have difficulty touching and loving one another. Somehow they have learned to become ashamed or afraid of affection. What a loss! What a shame! Not a day goes by that I do not smother my children with hugs, kisses and affection. While I would like to think that I do it for them, which I do try to do, the reality is that it is more important to me. Hugging, kissing, touching, and loving are essentials in my life, not unlike food, water and air.

The ability to touch and be touched is a wonderful sense that the body has given us to share and receive. Give of it generously. Learn to give hugs freely to family, friends and strangers. Do not be afraid to open yourself up and share physical affection freely. The next time you make love with your partner, dedicate an entire hour to the sense of touch, taking time to touch and explore each other. You will be amazed at the heightened sense of pleasure you will both give and receive.

To have a healthy body we must learn to appreciate that which the body has to offer. We learn this appreciation, first, through awareness and then by engagement. Become aware of your senses, focus your attention on them whenever and wherever you can.

By simply taking time each day, or ideally in each moment, to focus upon that which you are experiencing, you will fully engage your senses. As you do so, you honor and appreciate your body. As you honor and appreciate your body, so to will your body honor you, by giving more of that which you are appreciating. Your senses will come alive and your life will become filled with the richness and glory of your existence.

12.

Sexual expression between two lovers is a glimpse of the divine union of mind, body and spirit.

No discussion of the physical body would be complete without a discussion of sexual expression. Nor would it be as much fun. It is hard to think of a topic so important to so many people, yet rarely discussed openly, intelligently and inquisitively.

Sex, quite simply, is the closest many of us ever get to the ultimate, divine union of body, mind and spirit. Spiritual masters around the world often cite to the expression of sexuality between two lovers as the closest example we have of nirvana – the state of total and complete union with spirit. Sexual expression does this because it is one of the few things that we do in which we become completely present moment focused. As we sexually express ourselves we forget the past and the future and we allow ourselves the pleasure of focusing completely on the moment. And for that moment we become totally alive.

Many people regard sex, consciously or subconsciously, as the ultimate escape, and their engagement in sex is often pursued to avoid "the reality" of their lives. Sex, used in this way, becomes a pleasurable distraction from the unhappiness of their lives. "Real life" for most people is what they associate with the high drama going on in their lives - a collection of characters, places and events filled with all kinds of imagined and falsely perceived issues, problems and developments. In this version of "real life," time is most often lived in the past or future rather than in the present moment.

But for the precious time that most people spend in sexual union they escape this drama. Their worries become distant passing thoughts. Problems seem to melt away as the lover becomes absorbed into the rapture of ecstasy. Even time and perspective change during sexual bonding. The past and future become irrelevant and the exact present moment takes on a heightened importance. Time passes quickly and goes by unnoticed. Passion is expressed fully and emotions, instead of being repressed, enter the sexual arena. There is nothing like making love when you are emotionally charged in one way or another.

During sexual expression, all of our senses become employed and the moment is fully utilized and appreciated. Nothing else matters as we allow ourselves to absorb completely into our partner and the feelings and sensations we are experiencing. In essence, the unity of our self and our partner becomes complete.

When we are engaged in a sexual union with someone we love, everything becomes alive. We can smell the warmth of their breath, the fragrance of their body. We can taste the moisture of their lips and the softness of their skin. Taking the time to explore their body with our hands, we can feel the warmth and texture of the shape of each part. We can hear the depth of their breathing, the low tones of satisfaction our interaction causes, and the beating of their hearts. And with our eyes we see them completely, deeply.

In sexual union, our partners share themselves, opening their body, mind and spirit to us. As the senses become fully engaged, lovers encourage each other and feed on the energy of each other, building to a supreme moment of total and complete ecstasy: orgasm. When this moment finally occurs, every sense seems to explode and waves of satisfaction, pleasure and joy envelop our entire bodies.

Having these kinds of experiences it is no wonder that time becomes irrelevant. The present moment is experienced completely, and we feel passionate and alive. These intimate sensations, however, are not reserved exclusively for sexual union. They can be captured at other times by our awareness and appreciation.

Learn to appreciate and celebrate your sexuality. For long enough we have allowed others to make us feel guilty about loving sex, even though we do. It is natural to enjoy sex and it is natural to express our sexuality with someone who wants to share it with us. Sex is not something to feel guilty about, rather it is something we can have to make our physical, mental and spiritual experience more satisfying, more complete.

Because of all of the guilt, shame and fear we as a culture have attached to sexual union, we have created many "sexual problems" and "obsessions." We have also turned our priorities upside down. We live in a culture that tolerates our children viewing people kill each other and committing acts of violence against each other, but we dare not allow them to see people making love to each other. We think nothing of highlighting images of death, killing and violence every day on the news, but we dare not show an act of lovemaking.

Rather than allowing sex to be a natural way of expressing love for another or experiencing the physical sensations of our bodies, we have learned to use sex as part of our power and control games; as a distraction from our psychological or spiritual deficiencies; or as a consequence of our addictions and emotional deficiencies.

It is time to change this. It is time to adopt a new paradigm concerning sexuality: one that honors and celebrates sexuality. We ought to openly and honestly discuss the subject of sexuality and find in sex, beauty and joy, rather than shame and guilt. We need to learn to avoid using sex to exercise dominion or control over another; as a distraction from our problems; or to feed our egos.

The divine union that is created by two people making love to each other is the closest many will ever get to the experience of divine completeness or oneness. It is in the bond of sexual union with a loving partner that the sensations of our physical body become fully engaged, that our minds become completely present moment focused, and the rhythmic energy of our spirits becomes fully entwined with that of our loving partner. We become one with ourselves in mind, body and spirit, and we become one with our partner.

It is in these moments that we rise above our humanness, our apparent separateness, and we become, if but for a moment, fully enveloped by and in the divine power of the universe that is responsible for our very creation. Indeed, these are moments not to be ashamed of, or to hide, or to dishonor through our abuse of them. Rather, these are the moments we should celebrate, honor, cherish and hold sacred in our lives.

13.

In the end, our bodies are merely specific physical manifestations of the energy that exists in all life.

The last twenty years of science have produced an amazing

amount of information and discoveries about our bodies, about our life on earth, and about the universe in which we live. Interestingly enough, we have probably learned more about our universe and the explanation for our existence here on earth by turning our study inward, to ourselves, than by trying to explore space.

For this exciting information to help us better understand our being, indeed our soul, we must turn to the study of quantum physics. Quantum physics is the study of subatomic particles: the atom, its components, and their behavior. These structures, invisible to the human eye, comprise the building blocks of all matter. But as proven by modern physicists, these structures are much more than simply physical elements of matter. Their existence and their behavior speak volumes, not only of our bodies, but also of our minds and souls.

The physicist Fritjof Capra once said: "The philosophical implication of quantum mechanics is that all the things in our universe (including us) that appear to exist independently are actually part of one all-encompassing organic pattern, and that no parts of that pattern are ever really separate from it or from each other." As we shall see, this statement has profound implications on our understanding of mind, body and spirit and our connection to all things.

Whereas we used to be taught by science that all matter was comprised of atoms, electrons and neutrons, modern scientists now tell us that the smallest materials making up matter include such things as quarks and leptons. The most fascinating aspect of the discovery of subatomic particles, however, is that they are not made of anything. They are, to be quite blunt, simply mathematical patterns of energy. They are spinning bits of energy that we cannot see. They cannot be observed as matter, but rather present themselves only with traces of their past presence in a particular space, showing us that they have been present, but never really presenting themselves.

Although it is hard to imagine, science has proven that human beings, indeed all life, broken down to their smallest known levels are, in fact, nothing more than spinning, circulating, mathematical, patterns of vibrating energy. These mathematical patterns of energy can be, and are, affected by all kinds of forces that cause the energy to change its patterns of vibration. Most fascinating of all, however, is the fact that these particles are affected by, and alter their patterns and behavior depending upon, the intention of their observer. Thus, we have learned that the building blocks of life are connected to each other and to us by a force we are not yet familiar with.

In experiments, for example, where scientists attempt to measure either the position of particles or their momentum, they find that a particle will react differently depending upon the intention of the independent scientist who is conducting the experiment! In fact, it is now well established that the intention of the observing scientist must be taken into account when evaluating the outcome of subatomic experiments that attempt to measure particles, because that intention always has an affect on the action of the measured particle.

Science has learned that it cannot separate the intention of the observer from the action or outcome of that which is being observed. In other words, the thoughts and energy emanating from the observing scientist physically affect and alter the circulating, spinning energy of the particle being observed.

Thoughts, words, action, music or any other form of energy movement can and do have an effect on the movement and circulation of our energy. Moreover, our thoughts, words, and actions cause an effect on the energy of others and on the cosmic energy that surrounds us and forms a part of all life.

An example of this dramatic effect was shown a number of

years ago in a university study. Researchers took two colonies of monkeys and placed them on separate islands thousands of miles apart. The researchers then took one group of monkeys on one island and taught them specific tasks monkeys would not instinctively know, nor that they had ever seen another monkey do before. What researchers miraculously discovered was that within several months the monkeys on the other island, with no interaction between the groups, began to emulate the distinctive behavior taught only to the first group of monkeys.

The implications of such studies are enormous. How could learning occur thousands of miles apart, and relatively spontaneously in time between two distinct groups of monkeys? What force in the universe could have created such an effect thousands of miles away? Would the answers to these questions also explain why, for example, researchers in different parts of the world working on the same problem seem to "discover" the solution to a problem at the same time? Would it explain how civilization in different parts of the world evolved intellectually at more or less the same rate, despite no known interaction between such groups?

The answers to these questions I believe lie in the theory of vibrational life. I believe there are energy fields that exist both within us and around us, and they create a link between people, animals, plants and all life. These fields are not specific to a limited area, but rather are invisible fields of structured energy that ultimately transform themselves into molecules, cells and organs. This energy circulates, spins and gathers other energy to differentiate and specialize, thus creating unique differences within any particular life form. This energy has mind and soul, and when combined with other energy in a tightly condensed flow, forms matter. This matter ultimately forms all physical life. This energy flows through the air we breathe, the water we drink and the food we eat. It creates an invisible bond within us and between us, and all things. It is vibrational life and is the intelligent energy that is responsible for creation and evolution.

Here is an example of how it works. Let's assume we moved a breed of dogs to an area of the world where they were not indigenous. And perhaps in this area of the world they had a skin or coat that caused them to have health problems, rather than creating health advantages. The unconscious will (stemming from the discomfort) of the dogs would exert an influence on the energy field that connects these dogs. Over time, this energy, which ultimately bonds and forms the physical matter that is in the dogs, would initiate a change in the formation of the skin and coat that would be reflected increasingly in their subsequent generations of offspring. Adaptation and change, over time, would inevitably create a breed of dogs that more easily survives in that part of the world.

Our evolution as a species, and indeed as individuals, occurs not only as a product of natural selection and unconscious adaptation, but also because of "collective and individual will and intention." This will and this intention affects the energy circles that exist within us and that connect us to all things. This theory of vibrational life also explains certain aspects of social evolution. As we continue to improve on old ideas and use them to create new ideas and thoughts, we individually and collectively move the energy field of our species forward. As the forward-thinking author James Redfield states: "At any one time, the level of human ability and awareness can be thought of as being defined by the shared [energy] field. As individuals actualize particular abilities – running faster, picking up on others' thoughts, receiving intuitions – the [energy] field is shifted forward not just for them but for all other humans. That's why inventions and discoveries are often put forward at the same time in history by individuals who have no contact with each other."

Vibrational life and shared fields of energy also explain why some people have the ability to see into the past or future, or why some people seemingly recall circumstances and events from other lifetimes. Often people who have observed these abilities in others have believed such individuals to be miraculous, gifted, or depending upon their perspective, as possessing demonic powers. As Augustine once taught us, however: "Miracles do not happen in contradiction to nature, but only in contradiction to that which is known to us of nature."

Miracles, visions, and intuitions are, I believe, a person's unconscious or conscious ability to tap into shared fields of energy or vibrational life to receive or utilize information. As we become more attuned to our spirit, to our "inner selves," we gain the ability to tap into these fields of energy and utilize the vibrations contained therein to advance our own identity-specific energy pool, our own "individuality" if you will. As we open ourselves to our shared fields of energy and vibration, we open ourselves to a much greater collective power that can greatly enhance our own potential.

Vibrational life is consistent with modern scientific principles of quantum physics, which suggests that all life and life forms are simply different vibrations of energy. As we move or act in a particular way, as we vocalize our intentions and thoughts, and indeed when we even think thoughts, we create new energy and alter the existing energy that lies within and around us. What we think, say and do affects the universal pool of energy available to all. It is upon this vibrational aspect of life that the Law of Karma and the Golden Rule operate, providing us in return that which we contribute to the universal pool of energy.

What we think, say and do also affect our own specific well of energy, influencing the smallest particles of energy that comprise our nuclear structure. When we feed our "energy" with positive, loving, constructive contributions, we thrive and grow. When we feed our "energy" with negative, unloving, destructive contributions, we retard our growth and inhibit our ability to thrive.

We think of our bodies, minds and spirits as being distinct and separate, but they are not. The energy that circulates in our bodies is the same energy that flows through all life. It is the same energy that we use to formulate or receive thoughts and initiate action. It is also the same energy that is responsible for the creation of our spirits. It is for this reason that mind and spirit can so greatly affect our physical experience. This energy is the web that connects all life and that forms our oneness with each other and all things.

Mind

Being balanced means that we develop our minds as well as our bodies. The following section details the attitudes and behaviors of the mind that, once developed, will contribute to our balance of mind, body and spirit, and ultimately lead to our cultivation of real and lasting happiness.

1.

Scientists believe we are physical machines that, through experience and evolution, have learned to think. An enlightened person considers whether in fact we are thoughts that, through experience and evolution, have learned how to create a physical machine.

In India it is taught that if you want to see what your thoughts were like yesterday, look at your body today. If you want to see what your body will be like tomorrow, look at your thoughts today. The mind is a powerful weapon that we do not fully understand; its' thoughts reach far outside the confines of our physical bodies.

Quantum physics teaches us that the smallest existing particle is nothing more than moving energy. The confined mass of this moving energy creates matter. The more solid the appearance of the matter, the slower the energy contained within that matter vibrates. The higher the rate of vibration of the energy, the less solid appears the matter. We assume our ability to think comes from the combined collection of energy we call the mind and the body. But, perhaps, intelligence that can think is the energy that learned to create the mind and body.

Thoughts are nothing more than the intentional movement of energy. That is why every thought is important. Every thought moves energy and the movement of this energy affects us and all other energy. What we think affects all other energy much like a stone dropped in a giant pool sends ripples throughout it. Eventually the ripples meet the edge and bounce back toward their source. Likewise, the energy that we create and emit ultimately returns back to us. Do not take lightly, therefore, your words, thoughts or actions; they alter and affect the universe and the energy in and outside of you more than you can imagine.

"I am that, thou art that, all this is that, and that alone is."

The question this ancient vedic wisdom leaves us, of course, is what is "that"? "That" is intelligence, the universal energy that exists in all. The underlying and essential element of existence: source. You are intelligence, I am intelligence, and all that exists is intelligence. There is nothing else. Intelligence is what allows me to exist and know that I do. Intelligence allows me to live, to learn and to love. Intelligence allows me to think and create. Intelligence allows me to choose. Intelligence allows me to define myself and demonstrate myself to others.

You are intelligence and nothing more. But there is nothing greater in the universe than this intelligence, for it exists in all things and all things exist in it. As intelligence, you have the ability to manifest yourself as anything. You create what and who you are. You decide how you want your intelligence to be represented to others.

Understanding this principle is important, for it forms the gateway to true happiness. The real power of the mind is not in external learning, but rather in internal understanding. One begins to grow in knowledge and understanding when one ventures within, instead of constantly seeking without. Inside our very beings, we find intelligence and ultimately the keys that unlock the gates to wisdom and happiness.

Do you fully utilize the powers of your mind? Your mind will give up its secrets, but only if you know how to knock and have the courage and determination to enter. As many have said, there truly is no limit to the power of the human mind. But to truly discover its secrets, we must learn how to concentrate and focus internally.

As we know from our daily existence, it is far easier to focus our minds on external things. But how many of us turn the scrutinizing power of our minds on the mind itself? There is much to be discovered there. Like a dark room opened to the penetrating rays of the sun, if we learn to search within ourselves, we will find many answers hidden there; including some answers to the most fundamental questions of our existence.

Human beings have the right to ask "why" and to have their questions answered. But like answers to all hard problems, solutions do not always come easily: they often take significant time, effort and patience. If we take the time to search inward for our answers, I believe all can be revealed to us: including the keys to our own happiness.

2.

Only those with ears can hear.

We cannot and should not begin to make the changes we seek unless we have ears to hear. That is to say, we can search for answers to the questions we have, but to hear an answer we must be willing to accept it, even if it differs from our previously held beliefs. In other words, we must be open-minded.

It is easy to say we are open-minded, but what does that mean? I have yet to meet anyone who believes they are not open-minded, yet I know a lot of close-minded individuals. Being open-minded means that we acknowledge we are placing our interpretation on everything, seeing everything from only one point of space and time, one point of view. It also means we acknowledge that there are endless different points from which to view any thing and every thing, any one of which would necessarily change the appearance or interpretation of that thing.

Picture if you will a towering mountain far in the distance that you wish to climb. Before you embark on your journey to the summit, you pack your things. Among the items you bring is a camera with numerous rolls of film. As you start out on your journey you take a picture of your goal – the summit of the mountain.

As you continue your trek, at each milestone along the way you take out your camera and take a new shot of the mountain peak. Because your path winds around the mountain, taking you through different valleys, the shots you take of the mountain summit are varied, individually beautiful, and different. When you finally reach the summit of your mountain, you sit at the top, take out your camera, and take one final shot of the entire valley and trek that you followed to reach the mountain peak.

When you get home from your journey you run straight to the camera shop to have your pictures developed. As you look at each of the pictures, you remember clearly the view of the mountain you had when the picture was taken. You recognize that each photograph represents exactly the view that you had at each step of the journey. But you cannot help but notice how different each picture is, and how differently the mountain peak appears from each angle.

Each picture reproduces exactly the view you had at the exact moment in time and space that the picture was taken. They each represent one point of view of the mountain's summit, one point of space and time. But the pictures also illustrate the fact that there are endless different points from which to view the mountain peak, each accurate in their own right.

So it is with life. Life is like our journey up the mountain. Your thoughts and views today represent just one stop along the path. If you are moving and progressing, your thoughts and views will change. So too will your picture of the top of the mountain change. If you are not moving and progressing forward, then you, likewise, can expect that your thoughts and views have remained and will remain the same. Your view of the mountain summit will likely stay the same.

If you are learning, growing and progressing on your path, the thoughts and views you have tomorrow will be no less real or accurate than the ones you have today, no less real or accurate than the ones you had yesterday, and no less real or accurate than the ones that others have who are on different paths. They are all real and accurate views of the top of the mountain, just taken from different angles and perceptions.

Your understanding of the mountain's summit is greatest when you expand your perspective of it and you are willing to see it from different angles. This is when real learning begins.

Learning starts with suggestion. Somebody or some situation makes a suggestion to us and we choose whether or not to internalize it or teach ourselves something with it. The learning occurs within us by our agreement to accept the new idea and disregard our own differing perceptions of it, if any.

If we close our minds and reject any new thing because it disagrees with our prior notions or beliefs, then we are being close-minded and our learning will cease. Likewise, if we try to force all new ideas or thoughts into the shapes of our prior beliefs, then we will learn little or nothing. We must be willing to accept that new ideas can, and will, replace old ones.

To be truly open-minded we must be intellectually prepared to abandon old ideas when presented with new ones. Unless we are open to this process we will cease to learn. We cannot look upon new ideas solely through the vantage of our own thoughts and experiences. To be truly open-minded and continue a path of learning and progressing forward, we must force ourselves to look at new ideas objectively, as others with different experiences might view them, even if they challenge or would replace the very core beliefs we held in the past.

In essence, we must be willing to "unlearn" what we already know.

A college friend of mine used to work nights in a restaurant as a waiter so he could practice golfing every day. He wanted to become a professional golfer. Even though he was better than any golfer I knew and regularly scored close to par, or close to the score he would need to become a professional golfer, he was not good enough. To be a professional golfer he needed to get better. He needed to lower his stroke average (the number of golf strokes it takes to get around the course) by just a small margin, perhaps three or four strokes. So he decided to relearn the game of golf.

This was no easy task. He went to a new teacher who made him abandon his bad habits and many other things he had learned about golf over the previous ten years. His teacher made him start over. He was taught a new way to play a golf shot. For the first year following this new training his golf game actually got worse: his handicap increased to almost twenty strokes. But surely and steadily over time he improved until he finally reached a stage where he had improved his game enough to have a chance to make it on the pro tour. His success, however, came only because he was willing to set aside many of his previously held beliefs about golf and learn new ideas. He was willing to challenge and "unlearn" what he thought he previously knew about golf.

The same is true in life. To continue a path of growth we must be willing to challenge old assumptions and beliefs and relearn that which we may think we already know. This is something many people find very difficult to do. When science proves that a previously held religious belief is false, many religious people try desperately to interpret this new fact so that it fits into their belief system, rather than accept the fact that their previously held belief was simply incorrect.

The open-minded approach to life, however, requires that a person be willing to be wrong. Open-mindedness requires you to consider and accept that new facts may prove old facts and beliefs to be untrue. Children learn and grow quickly because they are very open to new ideas and beliefs. To them, everything in life is new and different.

As people get older, however, unless they make a point of learning and exposing themselves to new ideas, it becomes easier to tread in routine and habit. Seldom faced with new ideas or beliefs, they forget the process of learning and become more cynical of new ideas that do not match their belief systems. Unless they learn how to learn again, and unless they are willing to challenge their own beliefs when presented with new facts, their learning ceases. One of the first steps towards realization of self and forming a stronger connection to soul, therefore, is a willingness to change and to consider new thoughts, ideas and actions.

If the thoughts, ideas and actions of your past have not made you truly happy, if they do not truly represent you, then you must be willing to change them! What have you got to lose? Your old ideas and actions have not allowed you to be happy, so have the courage to try a new approach.

Allow your ears to hear.

3.

Happiness requires the acceptance of responsibility.

"Responsibility" says Deepak Chopra, "means not blaming anyone or anything for your situation, including yourself. Rather, it is the ability to have a creative response to the situation as it is now."

You must learn to accept responsibility for everything in your life. Too often people say that this happened to them and that happened to them. Everything is used as an excuse for what they have done or for what they have failed to do. As long as you falsely believe that there is someone or something doing something to you that prevents you from achieving more or doing something different, you deprive yourself of the power to do anything about it.

By accepting personal responsibility for your circumstances you immediately empower yourself with the ability to change those circumstances. Life is filled with countless examples of people who rose to the pinnacle of success out of the valley of horrific conditions. By accepting responsibility for their position and their conditions, these people moved forward relying upon themselves. Having accepted personal responsibility for everything, they were free to make positive things happen. A perfect example of this is the life of Nelson Mandela. Despite growing up in conditions of poverty and racism, despite being imprisoned for most of his life, he chose love as a reaction to these things, instead of fear. Leading a nation and becoming a respected world leader were the consequences of this choice.

Often I hear people say that this thing or that person makes them angry. Nobody can make us react in any way – only we choose our reactions. The continually happy and positive person is not happy and positive because every circumstance in her life is right. She is continually happy and positive because she chooses to react even to the difficult situations in her life with a happy and positive outlook. Anyone can feel good when life seems to be going right. However, the true master and the truly happy person is she who chooses to react to all situations in life in a positive way.

We must stop believing that people make us feel this way or that way. In truth, nobody makes us feel any way. We alone are capable of feeling any way, for we alone control, or fail to control, our emotions. I can choose to act rudely towards you, but unless you allow me to offend you, I have no effect. When you act in a hostile way towards me, I can choose to be upset or I can train myself to understand your actions and respond with love.

When we choose to be frustrated or angry with others, it is our bodies that suffer from the stress. It is our day that is ruined. So we must learn to control our responses by training ourselves to not react when others act toward us in a way that would normally upset us. The first step towards learning this control is to remember that we choose our reactions – and remember this when we begin to react or feel strongly a particular way.

Once you accept responsibility for your emotional choices and reactions – give yourself a break! We are all human and we all have lessons to learn. No one is perfect. We are imperfect beings struggling to find love, acceptance and happiness. In our quest for these things, we often make what I like to call "learning choices." Some people refer to learning choices as mistakes or sins, but that implies that the choices are wrong or bad, or should not have been made. Many times, if the learning choice is not made, learning does not occur.

Learning choices increase our experience and our knowledge about life and help us define what it is we want and who it is we want to be. Even the so-called "bad choices" are perfect examples and lessons of what not to do, instead of what to do. By learning what not to do, we also learn what to do – the opposite. So always remember that the learning choices that you continue to make are a necessary part of your growth and development. For that reason they are to be recognized and embraced, and appreciated for what they are: stepping stones on your path to becoming truly happy.

Accepting responsibility for every circumstance in your life and recognizing that your life is, and has been, completely your spiritual creation is one of the first mental steps you must take on the road to happiness. However, you do not need to feel bad about yourself. Embrace every decision you have made in your life as a "learning choice," a necessary step to get you where you are today: on the path towards eternal love, happiness and peace. Learn to appreciate your learning choices, as they will provide you with the context from which you will appreciate the happiness that will soon fill your life.

4.

Make every thought and action a conscious choice.

Taking responsibility for our feelings and reactions is difficult because it is not how we have been raised. As children we are conditioned by parents who are most often reactive, and who allow other people's actions to make them feel either happy or sad. Thus we are given a model of learned behavior that teaches us that external things can and should affect our mental state of happiness. By recognizing, however, that we alone are responsible for our thoughts, emotions and feelings, we lose our excuse for unhappiness and we gain the power to become happy.

This is sometimes difficult for people to accept, and even more difficult for many to change. The change is difficult because it requires a significant amount of conscious effort. Most of us exist each day minimizing the amount of conscious effort we exert. We get stuck in habits and ruts and we repeat actions and thoughts with little effort. When questioned about the way we think or act, we often respond mindlessly, stating "That is just how I am" or "I was raised that way" as if somehow we do not have a choice in the matter. In essence, when we think or act mindlessly, we are living habitually. Habitual living is not living at all. It is only survival.

Now is the time to stop surviving and begin living. It is time to take control of your life and make choices about what you think, say and do, instead of allowing old habits to represent who you are. You must analyze every action you take, every word you speak, and every thought you have and decide whether these things really represent you. Are they what you really want to be? If they are not, then you must change them.

We alone are responsible for our thoughts, words and

actions and the consequences that flow from them. We must accept responsibility for them. Once we do we can begin to change them. We do this by recognizing when a thought, word or action does not represent us as we want to be. Right then and there we must consciously decide to avoid repeating that thought, word or action.

Before we act we must also decide whether our proposed action represents who we want to be. If not, we should not act. As we begin to do this more and more each day, our thoughts, words and actions will begin to change and soon will begin to represent the highest vision we have of ourselves. Going through this analysis will make every thought, word and action consistently represent the best in us and the most divine experience of who we are. Consistently representing ourselves as the highest form of what we want to be will inevitably result in immeasurable confidence about who we are. This cannot help but make us happy.

Too often people are unwilling to change the way they think. Or they do not know how to view life's challenges as opportunities. When presented with a difficulty in life, they wonder what they have done to deserve such misfortune. We can change our thought processes. Like all learned behaviors, however, it takes time and it takes a process.

The first thing you must do to change the way you think is recognize the difference between how you presently think and how you want to think. When faced with a difficult circumstance, analyze your reaction and be honest about the emotion you have experienced. Look at the emotion objectively and do not react negatively if it is an emotion that you believe you should not have. You must accept the way you are today without judgment. The way you think and the way you are is neither good nor bad. It simply is. That does not mean you cannot wish to change your reactions or thoughts. You should consciously decide who it is you want to be and be willing to make changes if necessary. But make such changes without judgment.

Next, try to look at the problem differently. Think consciously about the kind of reaction you would want yourself to have. Then, try mentally to adopt that reaction. For example, let's say that you wish to change an angry reaction you feel when your partner does something that normally annoys you. First, recognize the emotion of anger that you typically feel. Accept the fact that anger in many situations is even a good thing. Understand that this reaction does not make you a bad person, it is simply is a response you wish to change in this type of situation. In your mind, picture the angry response as an object that you are wearing. Then, mentally take it off and get rid of it. Now picture in your mind the response you want to have as a new object that you can put on and make a part of yourself - and put it on. Try to see and feel what it would be like to respond to the situation with this new emotion. Make the new emotion become a part of your response. The next time you are presented with an issue or challenge that brings up your anger, try responding with the new response.

Like any new behavior or action this process of change takes time. So be patient and focus on the process itself, not the results. You will make mistakes or "learning choices" and, at times, slip into old habits. However, as you continue to focus on this process of change and the reactions you want yourself to have, it will not be long until you will become the person you are trying to be.

Do not get down on yourself for acting in ways you believe are wrong. Even when it seems clear that you have acted in a way that is less than your potential, have faith that on another day, perhaps tomorrow, you will choose to represent yourself as the highest expression of what and who you really are. Have faith that you will learn from your mistakes today. Have faith that tomorrow you will act only out of love.

5.

The happiest person is the person who has learned to be honest with himself.

As children we are often taught the importance of being honest in our dealings with other people. We are taught that it is improper to lie or be deceitful in our relationships. While undoubtedly this is a valuable principle of life, we are often not taught the value of being honest with ourselves.

Through the process of correction and discipline, children learn implicitly that they should strive to make others happy. We when do wrong things our parents become unhappy with us and try to correct our behavior. When we act the "right way," our parents express their pleasure with our actions. Through this behavioral training we grow up always trying our best to please others - and we often lose ourselves in the process.

To become truly happy, however, we must learn to be honest with ourselves.

Being honest with ourselves may sound easy, or may sound like something we already do, but in truth most people struggle with this. That is one reason why so many people are unhappy. Few of us rarely put into practice all that we believe. As a result, most of us are stuck in varying degrees of being unauthentic. Whether it is your work, your relationships, your religion, or any of your associations, ask yourself if you feel comfortable presenting exactly who you are in every situation you are in and with everyone with whom you associate. Ask yourself whether there is anything you do that you would not want some specific person in your life to know about. If you cannot be exactly who you are or cannot share everything about your life with the people you associate with, then you have an issue with authenticity or personal honesty.

Authenticity means having a very close alignment between who it is you really are, and what it is you say and do. The more closely aligned you are, the more authentic you are, and the more happy you are likely to be. The less closely aligned you are, the more unauthentic you are, and the more unhappy you are likely to be. You may understand many things, but unless you put into practice that which you believe, you are not being authentic. And if the rubber is not hitting the road, then you will not be happy and your wheels will spin.

The first step towards becoming mentally honest with yourself is conducting an honest evaluation of your life. This means asking yourself some really tough questions about what it is that makes you truly happy. For example, are you doing a job or are you in a career that makes you really happy? Is your partner a person you respect and are proud of? Does your religion represent your views about God? Do your friends nourish and sustain you and represent values that you believe are good?

Often we end up in careers, relationships, friendships, or religions that others, like our parents, think would be good for us. For a few moments of approval from others, we sacrifice a good part of our waking day being that which actually makes us unhappy – and then we wonder why we are unhappy.

To become truly happy, you must align your personal values and your real motivations with your daily life. For example, we spend too much time each day defining ourselves by our work. Your work, therefore, must be that which represents the real you. Spend time to define for yourself what is really important to you. Do you want to help people? Do you like to interact with people? Do you value security over freedom, or vice versa? What do you want to accomplish in life? Once you answer these types of questions, then begin to investigate whether or not your job fulfills these values. If not, look for other jobs that might. Perhaps this might mean more training or education, but that is a small price to pay for happiness.

If there are no jobs that fulfill your values, then consider creating something on your own that will. If you can be successful doing something that does not represent you or make you happy, just think how successful you can be doing something that you really believe in, something that does represent who you want to be. Being honest with yourself about what makes you happy, and then making changes to align your behaviors with your beliefs will bring lasting satisfaction to your life.

The same is true of our relationships. Too often people exist in relationships that do not make them happy. Either they compromise too much of themselves in an effort to please the other person, or they spend too much time trying to mold the other person in to something that will please them. Either way, unhappiness will surely result for both parties.

When we betray our true thoughts, feelings and actions in an effort to please the other party and preserve the relationship, we compromise ourselves and we inevitably become frustrated and unhappy with our lives because such relationships are built on dishonesty. We are being dishonest with ourselves and with our partners. Sooner or later, such relationships are destined to fail, as we will become insensitive to them. True intimacy in a relationship cannot exist where there is dishonesty because in a dishonest relationship we hold back a part of our true self. This holding back is a block that will prevent true intimacy from forming in the relationship.

As difficult as the course of self-creation can be, you must begin to be honest with yourself as to what makes you truly happy, even if it causes disruption in your relationships, your work, or your associations. By deciding to be your true self, you will begin to align your actions and thoughts and you will become authentic. You then provide an opportunity to those around you to reject or accept your true self. If they accept you despite the changes you have made, then you know that they truly love you for who and what you really are. This can only make you feel happy, secure and loved.

If those around you reject the real you, then what does that tell you about the state of those relationships or associations in the first place? It tells you they were based on conditions and the perceived love within them was not real. Although it will be painful losing some of these relationships, by being yourself, in time you will attract those who will value you for who and what you really are. These relationships will bring true happiness to your life, for they will honor you and allow you to be yourself.

Personal honesty is, in reality, an issue of self-love. If you have difficulty being one hundred percent honest with yourself and those around you, then you cannot love yourself completely. It signifies that there is a part of you that you do not love, or that you despise, and your shame about that part causes you to hide it from others with dishonesty. To become truly happy and at peace with yourself, you must learn to resolve the personal honesty issue. This can be done either through the abandonment of the trait or actions that cause you to be ashamed, or by having the courage to own up to that part of you that you have tried to hide. This is an act of self-love, and it will bring you happiness. Being honest about who you are is simply saying to yourself and to others that "what I think and feel is good, it is me."

Honesty is about love and acceptance of self. By accepting and loving ourselves first, we allow others to accept and love us as well. If you do not love and accept yourself, how can you expect others to do it? Whether it is your work, your relationships, your religion, or your associations, you must begin now to be yourself.

The people who are most attractive in this world are those who are authentically and genuinely themselves. These qualities strongly attract others because they are so rare and because we always know where we stand with such people – for better or for worse. Thus, we feel secure in their presence.

The dishonest person often hesitates to express an opinion on any subject where they anticipate a contrary response from whomever they are with. Yet, whether we agree or disagree with an individual's position on a particular issue is usually irrelevant to how we feel about them as a person. Rather, how we feel about someone and whether or not we respect them is a result of their integrity and willingness to stand up and be counted for who and what they really are. As someone once said, "even the slug is a star when he decides to be his slimy and horny self."

Being genuine is the difference between a "loveable rogue" and a "liar or a thief." Some of the world's most famous criminals of fact and fiction, people like Robin Hood, Jesse James, or Zorro, although they were all criminals, were loved in part because they never pretended to be something that they were not – they were rogues and they openly declared themselves as such.

Define yourself as you are and want to be, and let the world see the real you. Ironically, you will not need the acceptance of others when you have learned to be honest with yourself about who you really are. In being you, you will become confident and you will attract those who will value you for what you are – an authentic and genuine person.

You will become you and being you will make you happy. I promise.

6.

One of the greatest obstacles to mentally achieving happiness and love is judgment.

Along the path towards becoming truly happy you will undergo many personal changes, be exposed to many different beliefs and ideas on the subject of how to obtain happiness, and will encounter many different people (some who you already know) who may condemn you for the choices you are making. As a result, their negative judgment and perhaps your own negative judgment may likely be the greatest mental obstacles you will have to overcome to achieve true happiness.

As we have already discussed, from a very early age we are trained to conform. As children we are rewarded for conforming behavior and punished for non-conformance. As teenagers and adults, others constantly tell us what is acceptable behavior and acceptable beliefs. When we conform ourselves to these opinions, we receive acceptance and tranquility. When we oppose or reject these opinions, we seemingly cause disruption and rejection often results.

Consequently, there is literally a cultural or social opposition to our becoming happy, by being who we really are. In truly making ourselves happy, many times we are forced to take positions or do things that oppose the opinions of those that are close to us. Rejection by them usually follows in one form or another, and because we are so often externally focused and so much of our self-esteem based on the acceptance of others, our personal state of happiness is disrupted.

We must learn to let go of the approval of others. We must learn to recognize that other's displeasure, anger or disappointment with us is the result of the fears and insecurities they have with themselves, projected on us. Being who we really are, when it is at odds with those around us, causes others to question themselves and come face to face with their own beliefs about themselves. This is a scary place for many people, and as a result, they often react toward us in an unpleasant or unsupportive way as a defense mechanism. If they can point out a problem with you, it takes the focus off them. We cannot, therefore, put too much value in the opinion of others, for their opinion is usually loaded with their own issues. Besides, they do not have to live your life, you do. So have the courage to be who you are.

To become truly happy we must stop being judgmental. "Well" you may ask, "how can I not make judgments based on my experience? Every day we all make judgments about many things – the clothes we wear, the friends we choose, and the actions of others." The first step towards eliminating judgment from our life is realizing that there are very few things in life that are inherently good or bad, right or wrong. Furthermore, most judgments in life are based on incomplete facts. Let me explain.

Our culture assumes a difference between the man who, trying to appease the hunger of his family, takes money from another so he can buy food for his family, and the man who at the direction of his military superior kills people. On the chest of the latter we pin medals, call him a hero and we honor him. On the chest of the other we pin the label of criminal and we punish him. The difference between the two is what we as a society deem as acceptable behavior. But what if it was the other way around? What if there existed a society where stealing to feed a hungry family was acceptable behavior, but killing for political reasons was considered evil?

The definition of our morals, of what is considered good and right, and what is considered bad or wrong, is dictated by the society and culture in which we live. They are rules and opinions that have evolved over time based upon the beliefs, religious or otherwise, of those in power. But they are only that. They are not necessarily universal truths, or universal rights or wrongs. If they were universal truths, they would be the same for all cultures and peoples, and they are not.

Let me provide an example. If a man kills another as a result of war, we say the act of killing is okay because, even though he killed another, he acted in compliance with a government order. If, however, a man kills another to take something from him, then we judge the act of killing to be wrong, because we do not approve of his intention for the killing. But rarely, if ever, do we judge killing in and of itself to be morally wrong. Even those most opposed to killing, will agree that there are times when it might be justified, such as in the protection of family members.

Most of our judgments are made about what we perceive to be the intention behind an action, rather than the action itself. But how can we ever know the true intention behind any action? Despite all apparent evidence, how can we ever really know for sure who has acted with pure intent and who has acted with evil intent? Furthermore, who does not believe their cause is just? Who are we to agree or disagree that any person's cause is just or not, when we can hardly know any of the thoughts they have had, or any of the experiences they have endured prior to committing the act we presume to judge correctly? Our individual experiences are so varied, so different, and so complex, how can we ever be comfortable judging the actions of another? And how can we judge another without knowing, as a fact, their true intentions? The answer is that we cannot.

Before you are to quick to make judgments about the choices or life of another, remember that reality is like watching television. If you only ever received one channel on your television set, you would be convinced that what you saw on that station represented reality. For example, people living in communist countries during the cold war had only one very distinct version of the news of the world that was presented to them. Unable to receive other views or other channels, such individuals were easily convinced that the view of the world they received was one that accurately presented the "facts."

But as the cold war melted, these same individuals began to be exposed to CNN and the BBC and other news stations that presented a different picture of the world than the one to which they had previously been exposed. They began to see a totally different picture, a totally different reality, than the one that had been portrayed to them. The same is true for us. How many of you regularly watch the news channels of countries like Russia, China or Cuba? Probably very few. You must understand then, that the reality of the world that is presented to you, to us, is not reality or truth in fact. Rather, it is simply one view, one perception of certain facts.

Life as many of us experience it, is like watching one channel on the television. When you begin to receive other channels, you quickly learn that what you have been watching and believing may not have been the complete picture. You gain the gift of perspective. The life station to which you have been tuned convinces you that it is real. Many have only ever watched a single channel and for them it is easy to dispute the reality of another. In fact, they are watching one channel of many and it only appears real for as long as they stay tuned to it.

By changing channels you learn that reality is relative, and that judgments and choices are relative also. The differing judgments and choices of another are no less real or "right" than your own, they are simply based on a different channel or experience. You cannot make a judgment about someone else's choices until you have been tuned to their channel for as long as they have and gained "their perspective."

Sir Francis Bacon once stated in jest that old people "object too much, consult too long, adventure too little, and repent too soon." Over time, people's continued exposure to a single channel can lead them to these debilitating traits. But Sir Francis Bacon was wrong in one respect – it is not a function of age that leads to these traits, but rather a function of ignorance.

In your life, choose to consider, not object. Choose to listen, not judge.

It is easy for us to condemn the practices of other cultures or people whose choices many times we do not understand. But how often do we stop to question our own attitudes, our own morals, or the values that we embrace? For example, we cannot understand cultures that choose to allow their elderly to end their lives in the avoidance of pain, yet many of us do not question the killing of our youth that occurs when we send them to battle over land or oil. We cannot understand how another culture permits a man to marry several wives, but we do not question our own culture that allows a man to have children by several women without the commitment or the responsibility of caring for them. We live in a culture that condemns the open exhibition of two people making love, but promotes violence and killing through the media or in our entertainment.

We must stop casting stones at others and begin considering our own actions and values. What do we stand for? Do we really agree with the values and judgments of the society in which we live, or do we merely accept them because we have never thought otherwise?

So many people seem confidant that their beliefs represent truth, while the beliefs of others represent error. But before you judge too quickly or too harshly, look closely and objectively at your own beliefs. Undoubtedly your beliefs include concepts that may seem normal to you because you have been raised to believe them, but to others they may seem crazy, weird or different.

When people reject their old beliefs and accept ours, we often say they have passed from error to truth. However truth does not come from error – it comes from truth. In all things, in all ideas, lie the seeds of truth. They are only, at times, difficult to see. But the soul in its journey passes through different stages, with each stage true at that time for that soul. The only thing that changes is enlightenment – the depth of our understanding. As we gain more experience, our understanding increases and we begin to see things differently. It does not make our prior beliefs untrue; they were only different views from a different point in space and time.

We cannot judge the actions or path followed by another, for rarely do we know the intent of their hearts. We cannot even fairly judge our own circumstances, for we do not know where they will ultimately lead. What may appear today to be a failure cannot be declared one until its outcome is final. For a perceived failure, in fact, could lead to more success. It is enough for us to try to understand the path we are following, learn to make wise and understanding choices, and love unconditionally. You do not have time in your life for idle judgment that by its very nature is premature.

The ideas of wrong and right, good and evil, are even more complex than they first appear. You may believe good and evil to be different, but in reality they are really just different manifestations of the same thing. Good and bad rely upon each other and in fact are eternally bound in dependence on each other. Without one we could not have the other. Without what we call "bad," we could never recognize or appreciate good. Furthermore, that which is good today may be bad tomorrow and he or she who acts badly today may act good tomorrow. There is nothing that is **intrinsically** good or bad. Like every being and every thing, there is good and bad in all.

The small earthquake that strikes and kills my friend I might call evil, but if it prevents a much greater earthquake that would likely have killed thousands of people we could call it good. Several years ago a mother drowned her children in the back of a car by rolling it into a lake. Many believed the act was pure evil. However to label it as such is to ignore the positive impact that every action will have if we look hard enough to find it. News agencies months after the event reported how thousands of parents all over the world reported feeling closer to their children, and how many made more of a special effort to comfort, love and protect their children as a result of this event. So is the action itself entirely bad or evil?

Although the actor may have acted with evil intent, the action itself cannot be so easily judged. Unless we know the full impact, both good and bad, of any action – how can we judge it? Good and evil belong to the relative world. Both are necessary parts in our experience. Both give us experience, teach us, and make our understanding more complete. Therefore, that which we would condemn should be appreciated as much as that which we bless.

There is a good reason why all the great masters teach us not to judge things. How can we do it? We may think it is easy to judge something as good or bad, evil or divine. But the truth of the matter is that everything changes, everything and everyone is complex, and what is good for one may be bad for the other. Of what worth, then, are our judgments?

The philosopher Osho once wisely said: "Whenever you say, 'this is beautiful,' you have brought ugliness into the world …Whenever you say, 'this is good, right, or moral,' you have brought immorality into the world, you have brought the devil into the world. In deep silence when you don't know what is good and what is bad, you don't utter any labels and names, in that silence the duality disappears. The world becomes one."

When we make a judgment about a person or thing, the only fact that is clear is that we are being close-minded and ignorant. I am often amused when I hear people talk about other people. "Oh" they will say, "he or she is a really nice person." "Do you think so," says someone else. "I heard this or that about them, and I don't think they are very nice at all." The truth of the matter is that they are both good and bad. So are you. So am I.

I should not be deceived to believe that anyone with whom I interact acts exactly the same way to all people with whom they interact. The way a person interacts with me will never demonstrate the complete person, for it is possible that although she treats me badly, she acts sweetly and lovingly towards others. Would it then be fair for me to say that she is a bad person?

You cannot judge me and I cannot judge you because neither of us sees the sum of the other. I only can see what you show me and you can only see what I show you. That is not all there is, and therefore it is inadequate for either of us to make declarative judgments about the other's "character."

Our differences should be our cause for celebration, not our reasons for disliking or judging one another. The differences between us are the very essence of life and our existence, for it is in these differences that we learn and grow. How much new understanding would we develop if everyone were exactly like us?

One of our eternal objectives must be, not the destruction of variation in the conditions of life, but rather to recognize unity in spite of these variations. To recognize that God exists in each of us regardless of our condition, and despite differences that we may not understand or that we may fear. Our goal must be to acknowledge infinite strength as the property of all despite apparent weakness, and to recognize the eternal, essential purity of the soul in spite of everything that may appear on the surface to the contrary. To accomplish this goal is to approach the divine.

Every great teacher has taught us to focus on goodness in people, rather than on our differences. In every person there are divine qualities, and the great masters do nothing more than help every person call forth that divinity within them. These masters see no differences – no color, no sex, no birthright, no level of affluence – they only see the divine. That is the reason why people either love the masters or hate them, accept them or reject them. Their pure love either touches our souls, or illuminates our hate and prejudice.

Before you judge another – remember one thing: the only difference between you and I, between men and women, between animals and angels, people and plants, and all living things, is our own personal expression of the universal power from which we all come. You and I are both outlets of the same power: God. Your nature is divine and so is mine. You may be considered by all to be an angel, and I may be held to be the lowest form of life. Nevertheless, my constitution comes from the same infinite ocean of existence, knowledge and potential as does yours.

In the darkness of night a figure in the distance can be seen to be a ghost by a superstitious person, as a mother by a lost child, as a criminal to a policeman, or as a friend by someone waiting for theirs. In all cases, however, the figure in the distance does not change - only the apparition changes in the mind and perception of the onlooker.

Be careful of the judgments you make about anything, for we live in a world of darkness. It is dark because ultimate truth requires complete knowledge and none of us has complete knowledge. The very fact of our earthly existence denies this completeness. Our judgments, therefore, are like the observer in the night: they reflect ourselves more than they reflect the true nature of the object we are judging.

Despite what you may think and despite what you may be told, you never know a person's real intent. We may believe we know it from our discussions with them, but we never know if we are receiving the full picture. We should not question intent. And we should not question choices. We must simply observe them, and when and if it is appropriate, present others with an opportunity to see a different path and a different choice. This is the path towards true happiness and love.

7.

Real satisfaction comes not from distraction, but rather from total awareness.

We live in a culture where it is easy to become distracted. We are bombarded with cultural, technological and entertaining stimuli every day. The majority of these stimuli are intended to grab our attention, and they do so by heavily focusing on one or two of our senses – usually sight or sound. Our modern lives have become so distracted by these outside noises that it has become difficult to listen to ourselves. With sensual bombardment a part of our daily lives, we often lose the ability or the desire to actively engage our own senses.

In our hearts and our spirits, however, we know intuitively that these cultural distractions are shallow and fleeting. They are distractions that take our awareness away from that which is real and meaningful. True meaning is usually found in that which lives – animals, plants, trees, nature, our spirits, our passions and our relationships. These are the things that provide us with true and enduring happiness. When we become aware of real things and we learn to appreciate real things, our happiness grows. So, too, grows the quality of our lives.

The more time we spend with distractions the less satisfied we become. No better example of this occurs than on a Christmas day for many western children. They wake up Christmas morning to heaps of presents and packages. All kinds of toys, presents and neat gadgets await them. And while these toys and presents can entertain them for a short time, it is not long, often only a day or two, until the gifts are abandoned and the children become bored. The best Christmas presents children are ever given are the real ones. Any parent who has ever given their child a brand new puppy or kitten Christmas morning knows this. This is a gift of life that is real.

Anyone who has sat atop a mountain watching a sunrise or sunset can testify to the fact that real experiences create real happiness. The problem, however, is how does one duplicate the type of experience you have while watching a sunset when you are stuck in the middle of a busy, working day? What can we do?

We must first realize that it is not just the experience of sitting on the top of a mountain that causes us to feel real and connected. Rather, it is that we allow ourselves to feel wonder and awe, and we focus on these, when we are sitting on the top of a mountain. In other words, we take the time to appreciate and notice what is awe-inspiring. When placed in new or unusual environments, we become more willing to open ourselves to our senses and awareness and allow ourselves to become present-moment focused.

However, we can learn to find awe-inspiring moments in our daily lives no matter what we are doing. To do so, we must simply become present moment focused and become aware of the beauty of life that is unfolding around us. At any point in your day, wherever you are, you can stop and ask yourself what each one of your senses can then detect and appreciate from the present moment. I often do this wherever I am. I turn my awareness to my senses and take time to consider each one, to discover what each one is feeling or sensing. During these moments, I feel a sense of wonder and awe about life and I see great value in the present. It is as if real life is once again captured and the past and future become irrelevant. All that is important is what is happening right then and there. Awareness becomes completely focused on that present moment, and appreciation inevitably follows.

The more we can become aware of and appreciate present moments, the more life fills our sense of value. When we become present moment focused and aware of all of our senses, we begin to have a new appreciation for life. We become less dependent upon distractions in our life and more interested and absorbed in things that may have previously appeared uninteresting. In other words, we begin to find value in that which is simple. The sky no longer is just the sky, but rather becomes a collection of muted and blended colors and shapes that cast shadows and highlights everywhere. It becomes a bastion of different smells that comes to us via the breeze, and it becomes a sensation of warmth or cold that we can feel on our skin. The plants and trees no longer are simply plants and trees, but rather they become like dancers in the wind, and playgrounds for all kinds of life. We can smell their fresh fragrances, we can feel their varied textures, we can see the intricacies of their patterns and shapes, and we can hear the life that lives among them.

The world is a collection of wonders, much of which we fail to see. But this reality can return to us by a readjustment of our awareness. By simply paying attention to that which we have previously ignored, we can rediscover life, and in so doing, we rediscover ourselves. All of us have had the experience at some point in our lives of a change in awareness. Perhaps it was when we got married, or had our first child, or got our first dog or cat, or changed our job. Whatever the change is, we are often amazed at the number of similar people or circumstances that suddenly appear. It is as if the similarities suddenly come out of nowhere.

For example, to the new dog owner, all of a sudden it appears that many people have dogs. New dog owners often find themselves running into people everywhere who have dogs, or who are walking their dogs. The new parent also goes through this process of a change in awareness. Suddenly everyone seems to have a new baby. Everywhere the new parent looks, they see other new parents or expectant mothers. They begin noticing ads on television, on the radio, and in newspapers that advertise things for babies. They begin to hear in conversations much more discussion about children. They also find themselves suddenly forming new associations with other people who have children.

In these examples, life does not change. There were a lot of people with dogs and children before the new dog owner or the new parent got theirs. All things existed before the change in circumstances to the same degree that they existed after the change. The only thing that really changed was awareness. The new dog owner or the new parent began paying *attention* to these things. That which was once ignored now suddenly gets noticed because of *attention* and *awareness*.

Turning our attention and awareness to the things that are real and simple in life, and that make us feel alive, is a very important step towards creating lasting happiness.

8.

Let passion and enthusiasm be what first comes to mind when others think of you.

The one consistent message of "life teachers" everywhere is to have the courage to follow your heart. "Listen to what the voice inside of you is telling you to be or telling you to do," they say, "and let go of the fear that prevents you from pursuing your dreams." Becoming who and what you really are and doing what your heart is telling you to do has a very significant side effect – it allows you to become passionate and enthusiastic.

There is nothing more magnetic in this world than the person who approaches life with passion and enthusiasm. Seeing someone doing what they love to do is a true joy, and when we are blessed to observe someone pursuing their dreams with passion and enthusiasm it often causes us to stop for a moment and become absorbed in their passion.

Think of someone you know that is passionate and enthusiastic. The energy surrounding such individuals is always magnetic. They are always up to something new and exciting. When you are with them, you cannot help but become interested in their engagements. They are alive, dynamic, and contagious. And they are always positive.

Even with an unhappy person, it is easy to see the transformation caused by passion and enthusiasm. Take, for example, the person who leads a dreary existence doing a job they hate five days a week. When the weekend comes and they get the opportunity to engage in their favorite hobby, even the dullest of individuals becomes engaged, lively, and full of fun and laughter. In short, they become passionate and enthusiastic.

We can become that way by first focusing on the moment.

What can you appreciate about this moment in time? By beginning to guide your mind away from the past or the future, and focusing it on the positive aspects of the present moment, you will begin to feel more enthusiastic and passionate. Next, begin to let go of your fear and follow the whisperings of your heart. What is it telling you to do? If you are prompted to scream with enthusiasm, do so. Do not worry about what others may think. If you see someone you are prompted to speak to, follow the prompting of your heart and speak to the person. What do you have to lose? Even if they are not interested in speaking with you, you will have honored and validated your heart and feelings. Passion and enthusiasm as character traits will become your reward.

Too often we live our lives dampening our enthusiasm or passion for life because of what others may think. We become concerned that others will think we are wacky, or abnormal. Or worse yet, that others will pay attention to us and may notice something they do not like. Let go of the opinion of others. Have the courage to be an individual, to be different. Understand that no matter who or what you are, there will always be people who will be threatened by your presence. That is their issue, not yours. Your responsibility is to your self. So give your self the freedom to be passionate, spontaneous and free. Be wacky and let others be puzzled by your joy in life.

You can be enthusiastic and passionate about everything in life. Like everything else, it is simply a choice. If you cannot find your passion or enthusiasm, then consider carefully what you are doing or how you are spending your time. Surround yourself with the work, the hobbies, and the people that make it easy for you to become excited, passionate and enthused.

Life itself is a reason to celebrate. Every day that we are alive, that we can breathe fresh air, eat good food, exercise and use our bodies actively, revel in and enjoy the feelings and physical effects of our senses, share love with friends and family, make love with our partners, and pursue the greatest purpose in life we have for ourselves, is cause for great celebration. Embrace life and find your passion. Let go of fear and anxiety, and guilt, and anything else that blocks your enthusiasm.

Follow your heart and let the flame of your passion and enthusiasm burn bright, so all may see and feel the warmth of the light that you offer.

9.

Take it upon yourself from this moment onward to always look for and focus upon the magic in life, and do not accept limitations to your dreams.

The world is not as bad as you and I may sometimes think. We are the ones that choose to see its negatives. We create our own ghosts and demons and then we wonder why we cannot get rid of them. We call upon God to save us from evil, but we don't bother to help ourselves.

As we create our own demons, to rid ourselves of them we must de-create them. That is to say, we must begin to see the world differently. Once we change our perspective, our circumstances will undoubtedly change also. We will start to see the light, by **choosing** to see the light. We will rid ourselves of the darkness and demons by refusing to acknowledge their presence. This does not mean self-delusion or convincing ourselves that everything is exactly how we want it to be. It simply means that to fill our lives with positive and rewarding experiences, we choose to focus only on that which is positive about our conditions. From all negative circumstances, events or people we can find positive consequences.

I have traveled and lived amongst the very rich and the very poor of this world, and always the pain of both can be attributed to one thing: their outlook and attitude on life. How else do you explain the person who lives with his wife and four children in a wooden shelter, where the sewage flows openly through his yard and his roof cannot keep out the rain because of its large holes. Despite such circumstances he still manages to see life as magical and greets each day with a smile? Or how do you explain the man who need never work again, has palatial estates in several countries, has the money to go anywhere or do anything, yet whose life is filled with fear, negativity, and the inability to see beyond the "problems" that beset him? Such people exist for I have met both.

If you learn nothing else in life, know that each and every day you have the ability to decide the mood and attitude with which you will approach that day and the circumstances that will present themselves. We cannot always control those circumstances, but we can always control our reactions to them. Make a conscious decision to alter the way you think and feel. Take it upon yourself from this moment onward to always look for and focus on the magic in life. It is there, if you will simply allow yourself to see it.

When my son was little, he loved to hear the story of Peter Pan and how he could fly. I would read him the same story every day: about Tinkerbell, fairy dust, and how Peter and the Lost Boys would fight Captain Hook and the pirates. One day he dressed himself in assorted clothes – a belt, a scarf that he used as a headband, a wrapping paper roll as his sword – pretending that he was one of Peter Pan's helpers, fighting Captain Hook. As he was about to engage in his make believe battle, he came over to me and in his innocence asked me as sincerely as he could whether or not he could fly.

"Of course you can fly" I said, "just close your eyes and pretend you are flying around the room." "No" he said, "I don't mean make pretend – can I really fly?"

It occurred to me at that moment that my answer could affect the way he would perceive life. Although my natural reaction would have been to explain to him that people cannot fly, I believed this was the wrong approach. I felt I should not say no. What right did I have to impose my perceived limitations on him? How could I say no, when the truth of the situation was only that I did not know how to fly, not that it was not possible. So I told him that he could fly, if that was what he really wanted to do. Of course he was delighted by my response.

Many may think that this response was wrong and that I was setting him up for disappointment in the future. Perhaps they are right. But I could not overcome the thought that just because I believed that people could not fly, did not necessarily mean that **in fact** people could not fly. It simply meant that people had not yet figured out a way to do it. And so I told my son that he could fly, but to do so he would have to discover a way to do it. That answer satisfied him, and he committed himself to trying to find some pixie dust.

He has since forgotten that conversation and the desire to fly. But what has remained and what I have always tried to instill in him and my daughter is the belief that anything is possible. Just because something does not **appear** to be possible, does not mean that it cannot be done. It simply means that we have to think more creatively and imaginatively for a way to do it.

How often do we allow our prejudices, beliefs, or our skepticism to inhibit our imagination? Undoubtedly more often than we should. I am sure our progress in life suffers as a result. We need to rethink the way we look at life. We need to be skeptical, not of new or different ideas, but skeptical of traditional notions of "fact." Only when we step out of the box of traditional thinking can we truly discover novel ideas.

As a television advertisement for Apple computers once stated: "the people crazy enough to think they can change the world are the ones who do."

10.

To accomplish great things, we must not only act, but also dream, not only plan, but also believe. Our dreams and our beliefs define the upper limits of what we can achieve.

The dreamer in society is often criticized, ridiculed or mocked. But without the dreamers, where would we be? We would be without any technological, biological, or scientific discoveries. Most likely, we would still be in the Stone Age, unable to advance our culture. Dreamers, however, help us to escape our limitations, because they look beyond our paradigms. In short, they create new paradigms by challenging the notions of our old ones. In so doing, they lead us to new realities.

The critic of the dreamer is he who, because of his own inability to dream and achieve great success, feels threatened and smaller in the presence of the dreamer. So he attacks her in an effort to cut the dreamer down to his size. But the dreamer is unaffected by such criticism. She understands that the only limitation to her success is the limitation she herself imagines. She understands that by setting her expectations above all others, and refusing to acknowledge failure, her visions and dreams will come true. She may have to change the rules, she may have to experience many outcomes that are not the realization of her dreams, but in the end she knows she will manifest her vision.

Do not criticize the dreamer. Instead, reflect on that part of yourself that fails to dream as she does. Try to see the dreamer's dream. Allow your thoughts to be creative. Search for solutions to the issues that temporarily prevent your dreams from being realized. Discover your own dreams. Do not allow yourself to be limited by "conventional wisdom" or traditional notions, for they do not represent the outer limits of what is possible, rather they are merely the outer limits of past dreams.

Many people do not allow themselves to dream because they believe that God controls all things in life, including our direction. God does not. You are the supreme creator of your life and you alone decide its direction. God may have created our existence, but She gives us the ability to direct it. She does so because she understands that the direction of life is less important than the ability to choose that direction.

You alone must take responsibility for the life you are leading, for you have chosen it and you continue to live it under its present terms. If you choose not to alter the direction of your life with the circumstances you encounter, then your direction will not change. But if your life is not what you want it to be, do not despair. You have the power to change it.

Some people feel that life is about discovering new things about who we are. But this concept of "discovery" implies that our characters or circumstances are set beyond our control and are simply waiting for us to understand or discover them. To realize our full potential in life, it is essential that we recognize that life is not about discovering ourselves, but rather about creating ourselves. There is no part of us that is fixed or beyond our control. Each day we make decisions about who and what we are by the actions we take. Responsibility for who we are lies with no one other than ourselves. Each day we choose who we are by either confirming prior beliefs, reactions and actions, or creating new beliefs, actions and reactions to the circumstances that are presented to us.

Nothing requires us to react the way we always have or the

way we may instinctively feel. We have the ability to control 100% of ourselves, including what we believe are our instincts. By understanding that our lives are a process of creation we begin to take responsibility for our actions and our reactions. We begin to consider our behavior and whether it represents the type of person we want to be. When it does not, we should create new reactions and behaviors that better reflect who it is we want to be.

Every day we are faced with choices about the actions or attitudes we will take in response to circumstances that are presented to us. Often we do not know how to react. Or we may act out of fear or our insecurities. In either case, unhappiness is usually the result.

The next time you encounter a situation that requires you to make a choice about how you will respond, try the following: imagine that you are everything you want to be, that you are working at your ideal job and you have all the financial security you need, you have the perfect relationship, and you are totally happy with who and what you are. Now, ask yourself what you would do as that person if you were faced with the same decision. Would you act in the same way as you are thinking of responding to that situation? If your choice is consistent with your immediate reaction, then you can have faith that the decision is a sound one.

If, however, you would act or respond differently as that ideal person, then consider acting differently. Choose as your response that which the ideal version of you would make. Making choices in this way will ensure that you are acting as the higher and most divine version of yourself. As such, your decisions will come from love and security, and not insecurity and fear.

If you always decide to act in a way that represents the most divine version you have of your self, you will never make a wrong choice. Moreover, your choices will begin to transform you into a higher and greater manifestation of the person you ultimately want to become. As we are simply the sum of our choices, the more you act as this higher version of yourself, the greater the version of yourself you will inevitably become.

Spirit

When the body and mind are willing and able, the path is clear for spirit to emerge.

1.

"We are not the body. We are not the mind. We are the ones who have mind and body." Deepak Chopra

It is easy for us to recognize body and mind – we can see them and feel them every day, in every moment. But spirit is more subtle. Spirit puts itself behind less tactile experiences. Spirit resides itself within. With so much of our cultural focus on material things, on external things, subtleties of spirit are often lost, muted or ignored.

But spirit is everything. Body and mind are but unique and specific expressions or vibrations of universal spirit. Body and mind are vehicles by which the spirit learns of, and experiences, itself. Spirit is love and love is spirit. It is our essence, God's essence, and the essence of all life.

Spirit is sensitive and thus it protects itself. When we are not prepared for it, spirit recedes. When spirit is ignored, it waits. But spirit never leaves for it is our essence. When we begin to open ourselves to spirit, it emerges. When we begin to listen to spirit, it begins to teach.

The degree of spirit that you see in another person or even

in yourself is directly proportional to your level of awareness and your willingness to allow spirit into your life. Spirit is a humble guest that does not force itself upon us. Rather, spirit answers when we beckon it.

We are all created as spiritual beings, and we exist as and in spirit. No person, animal or thing has more or less spirit than you or I. We simply differ in our manifestation of spirit. Be wary of those who claim to be more spiritual than you, or who claim to be a "special messenger" of God. In truth, there are no "special" messengers of God. There are only those in whom it is easier for us, as individuals, to see God. And for everyone, that vision is relative to our own experience and spiritual path.

All beings are equal manifestations of God or spirit. If we chose to look for God in all people we would see Her touch and presence in the life of the poor farmer, the rich businessman, or the small child as much as any proclaimed "representative of God." Indeed, we would see Her presence in all that is.

The fingerprint of God exists in the heart and soul of every thing and every being. It is always there and all struggle to understand, feel, and express it. So what claim to superiority can there be? The most ignorant person can be as great a messenger of God as any that ever existed, and as great as any that are yet to come, when they unknowingly touch the spirit of another.

The difference in our spirituality is in how earnestly we look for God in all beings. Consequently, the truly spiritual being is not the one who easily **speaks** of God or spirit, but rather is the one who easily **finds** God or spirit in all things.

2.

The search for spirit must begin within.

Following the creation, the Gods convened to survey their works and marvel at the splendor of their actions. They were particularly pleased with their creation of woman and man, whom they had created in their own image. But the Gods became concerned that their creation would quickly learn their secrets and powers and would find a way to undo their grand achievement. So, they came together on the eve of the culmination to discuss where they would hide their godly-powers.

"I have created the waters of the world to cover the earth," said Neptune, God of the waters, "and stretch to its deepest and darkest spots. Let us hide our godly-powers in a single location at the deepest spot in one of my great oceans – people will surely never find our powers there."

"No" the greatest of all Gods replied. "We have instilled in men and women creativity and thought, and surely they will use these powers to discover a way of searching the deepest and darkest corners of your oceans, seeking answers to the questions they will have. If we put our powers there, people will find them."

"The world that I have created is a round sphere of molten lava and rock, with layer upon layer of substances that will prevent mortals from discovering our powers, should we decide to place them at the very center of the world" cried the maker of the Earth. "Put them there and our creative powers shall be safe."

"But" said the Great God, "we have decided to endow men and women with the ability to reason and learn. It will not be long until they learn how to use the Earth to fashion tools and treasures, and learn to utilize the resources of the Earth to further their goals. In mankind's journey, they will use the Earth to further their search for our powers and it will not be long until they begin to search the Earth itself. In time, if we put them there, they will surely find them."

"I have created the heavens to look down upon the Earth and the people living there" spoke the God of the heavens and stars. "People will be overwhelmed by the expansiveness of space and will be dumbfounded by the countless planets and stars. Let us put our powers in the heavens where surely people will not find them."

Once again the Great God spoke: "You underestimate the abilities and intelligence of humans. We have created them in our image. As they will find a way to the bottom of the oceans, or the center of the Earth, so too will they find their way to the heavens. And although the stars and planets are many, what shall we do if they use their powers of perception, intuition and faith that we have borne in them to discover the place of our god-powers? What then shall we do?"

The other gods listened intently. "They are all fine ideas that you suggest for hiding our powers from people. However, it is certain that some day people will find our powers and become like us - which was our intention. There is only one place where we may hide our powers where they will be safe for a long time to come. Hiding them in this place will ensure that people learn to utilize all of the abilities we have given them to discover these powers, and hopefully by then, they will have learned enough that they will not destroy our creation."

"We will hide our powers deep within each person. Men and women by their very nature will spend their lives searching everywhere for these powers, but they will struggle to look within. The simplicity of this solution will be that which will confound them."

The other Gods all nodded in agreement with the Great

God and the powers of the Gods were placed deep inside of each person – where they would remain hidden from most people for ages to come.

The philosopher Sivananda once counseled: "Look within. Within you is the hidden God. Within you is the immortal Soul. Within you is the inexhaustible spiritual treasure. Within you is the ocean of bliss. Look within for the happiness which you have sought in vain."

There are many voices that proclaim the path you should follow and the truth you should hear. But remember that the greatest voice of God and truth is not found outside of you, but rather is the still, small voice inside of you. The voice within is the loudest voice with which God speaks, but often is the hardest for us to hear, because we do not take the time to listen. This voice does not come from your mind; it comes from your spirit. Listen carefully to it and you will hear the words of God.

Every person is special and each moment in every person's life a treasure. While we sometimes romanticize other eras and people, in reality, there is no time more special than the present and there is no person more special than you or I. Although many people believe that God only communicates with a select few, this is not true.

God did not create us to be dependent on the thoughts and feelings of others. She gave us a mind to think and a heart to feel – for ourselves. It is time we stop relying on others to tell us about God. It is time for us to discover God and begin exploring our own thoughts, our own feelings, and our own spirit. For this purpose, God created us.

The path inward is through meditation, contemplation and prayer. Learn to spend time with yourself and with your feelings. Quiet, still time alone will help you focus your awareness on what is going on inside of you, where the heart and spirit reside. Each day, take time to clear your thoughts, the business of your mind, and try to get in touch with your inner spirit. Guide your awareness inside, and dwell on those thoughts or feelings that speak of a greater awareness of higher choices in life.

There are plenty of books, tapes and seminars that can teach you how to meditate and pray. Read such books, go to these seminars and learn to develop your inner voice. It is the voice that comes from God that is the only voice qualified to give you the clearest path to your divinity.

The spiritual master, wanting more than anything to know the truth, turns her sight inward to behold the wonder, truth and glory of God. She does not seek outside herself. She does not seek to find union with external forces. The spiritual master, instead, seeks to establish union inside, with the deepest part of herself, where lies a present-sense awareness. Where she can experience reality directly, without the cloak of interpretation or the filter of thought.

In this state of introspection, of union with self and spirit, the spiritual person finds God.

3.

The true essence of God is not found in symbols that represent Her, rather it is found completely in spirit and love, privileges of all.

True spirituality transcends all things in life, all people. No life is a failure; there can be no such thing as failure in the universe where there is life. A person may hurt themselves and others constantly; they may seemingly tumble and fall in every instance. But in the final analysis they are an equal part of the universal spirit, an equal part of God.

We should not make judgments about the differing paths

that people take in life. The path you or I choose to take will be different than the path of others, perhaps even longer. But if it is the way you or I must go to realize our full potential, how can anyone say it is wrong? Nor should we make judgments about who is progressing forward or upward. To do so we would have to have the ultimate perspective to know which way is up and which way is forward. Every soul moves in a different way. Life is not up, or down, or linear, but rather it is circular. All beings must go around to complete the circle – experiencing both seemingly low and high. But no one will be lost. Your path may be different than mine, but both paths will take us where we want to go. So, we need to learn to respect and honor each other's path.

Henry S. Haskins cautioned us that we must "treat the other man's faith gently; it is all he has to believe with. His mind was created for his own thoughts, not yours or mine." A truly spiritual being does not abuse or criticize any other person's beliefs or their symbols, or call their worship sin. The enlightened soul recognizes that all belief is spiritual. How can it be a sin, therefore, for any man or woman to use a belief or a symbol of any kind to realize their divine nature? It cannot even be an error. If one's worship leads to greater truth, how can it be either? We do not travel from error to truth, but rather from truth to truth, from elementary truth to enlightened truth.

Sometimes we hear differently from people who proclaim to know the word of God. Such individuals cite sacred records like the Bible as support for the fact that God uttered the words or doctrines they proclaim. Based on this support, they assert that all others are wrong in their teachings.

What kind of support is this? We all know that the very words they cite were not written by God, but rather by men trying to interpret what they believed God wanted them to say. These people, no matter how spiritual we may believe them to have been, were nonetheless human, and were subject to human prejudices and perceptions. They were limited, as we all are, by their own experience and knowledge. Add to this the fact that their sacred words were often written in different languages and have been further subject to hundreds of translations by people with their own prejudices, beliefs, and experiences.

Yet, despite all of this, many people seem willing to accept such words as the "literal" word of God. Many people are willing to put their faith in these "words," even over and above their own thoughts and direct experiences with God.

Words are only symbols of someone's experiences and thoughts about a particular subject. They are nothing more than an attempt to put into human terms and understanding, that which is not merely human or subject to complete human understanding. Do not underestimate, therefore, your own ideas, thoughts, beliefs and experiences. They are more important to your own personal development and spirituality than any book ever written. Books are useful because they can teach us, but do not overestimate them: they are not God's direct words to you. Only you can write such words.

Do you ever wonder why there are so many different images and symbols of God? Even within a specific doctrine or sect there are hundreds of different images and symbols. Why? Perhaps it is because we have difficulty focusing on anything without being able to visualize it. Images and symbols allow us to visualize a system of beliefs. These external constructs help fix our minds on the object of our worship. But remember that the image is not the Being. The symbols and the words we use to describe the Being should not become the objects of our worship or the focus of our attention. Rather, they should be used only to allow our hearts, minds and souls to focus on **becoming** that Being and emulating its values.

God is not found in symbols, but in fact, is found in life. Each and every day, in everything you do God can be found. Look for Her. Seeing God is not a passive experience, it is an active one. It requires our attention. When you begin to look, you will find God everywhere. You will find the spirit of God in a song, in a whisper, in a picture, in nature, or in the kind words of a stranger. And as you learn to notice God in all things, and appreciate the hand of God, you will begin to find Her more easily. Before long, God will be everywhere and all that you see, do, and say will be a reflection of this experience.

When a person begins to realize their full potential, they begin to understand that divinity and Godliness are traits available to all. They understand that they do not need religion and its symbols to find and focus on God, for they can see God in everything. One does not need a special day of the week to focus on God, unless one fails to focus on God the other days of the week. One does not need a symbol or a church in which to focus on God, unless one fails to see the presence of God in all things.

True religion does not exist in doctrines and dogmas. It is not what you read and believe that is spiritually important, rather it is what you **realize** that matters. Blessed are the pure in heart, for they shall see God – and they undoubtedly do – in all things.

This is salvation and the power of attaining it is within us.

We live and move in God. We find God in all things, in all places. Religious organizations with their creeds, doctrines and symbols have a part to play, for they can help us form the foundation on which we spiritually grow. But remember, no religion ever created God. Rather God inspired all great religions. And no religion ever created a soul. The true destination of all religions, whether they understand it or teach it, is the realization of God in the soul. This is the one universal religion.

If there is one universal truth in all religions it is here: realizing God. Although the teachings and doctrines of religions may differ, and although there are seemingly thousands of different roads to God, if they are followed as far as they can reach you will discover that they all converge at one central point – the realization of Godliness.

You may believe in all religions, attended every church, know and understand all sacred books, but if you have not realized Godliness, then you are no closer to God than an atheist. Likewise, you may have never entered a church or a mosque, ever read a religious or sacred book, or ever participated in religious ceremony, but if you feel God within yourself and you aspire to divinity to the extent that you are lifted above the vanities of this world, then you are truly a holy person.

As soon as you stand up and say that you are right and your church is right, and all others are false or wrong, then it is clear that you are farther from divine truth than those you unfairly judge. Your declaration of separation demonstrates your lack of knowledge of God. Exclusivity and separation come not from God, but rather from the insecurities of man.

God does not separate; God unites. True divinity teaches the Godliness in all things and finds the divine in all persons regardless of beliefs or creed. True divinity understands the oneness of all life. The truly spiritual person understands that the divine purpose of life is the realization of God, the realization of oneness, regardless of the path chosen to reach it.

4.

The real nature of God is recognized by freedom of will and thought.

For many people, religion provides them with their beliefs

about God, life, death, morality, and many other issues of existence. This supply of information is useful for it provides them with standard answers to many questions about life. With such a steady stream of information about their existence being fed to them almost intravenously, however, some lose the ability to think independently, or they never develop it in the first place. They become or are dependent solely on the thinking of others.

Undoubtedly it is easier not to think for ourselves. It is easier to place our salvation in the hands of someone who guarantees to take care of it for us. Religions often promise to do this. Unconsciously, this is the attraction of religion for many. However, we cannot grow or expand our knowledge, understanding and experience by entrusting others with the most precious gifts we have been given: the ability to think and create, and the free will to make our own choices. Yet so often these are the gifts we relinquish most easily. We readily allow others to think for us, make our decisions and take away our choices, responsibility and our free will.

The stealing of our minds and our free will is never blatant. It is always positioned as "instruction" from spiritual leaders who are allegedly more in tune with God than the average person. Or, in the case of free will, it is positioned as the fact that we are free to make choices, but we cannot avoid the eternal punishment that attaches to wrong choices. But, of course, the bottom line is we lose the ability to think freely or make choices for ourselves. The inducement we receive from religion for giving up these precious gifts is what they prominently offer in return: acceptance. Religions are exceptional at adopting into the family those that "accept" their doctrines. Some will even call us "brother" or "sister." All make us feel a part of something grander than ourselves.

Despite our reservations about the doctrines they try to have us accept, and our subconscious struggle with the loss of our independent thought and free will, we feel secure and accepted in our new found family and we quickly overcome our loss. However, this acceptance is often conditional. Should we begin to question the thoughts or judgments of the religion's spiritual leadership, we find our status and our acceptance threatened.

What kind of love and acceptance is this? It is not unconditional. And if it is not, how can it be the pure love of God? How can it even claim to represent God's interests? Do not easily give up your gifts of free thought and free will. Hold them dearly, and resist the temptation to trade them for security and acceptance. The only acceptance that is worth anything is the acceptance of yourself, by yourself. Do not worry, God will not abandon you. The unconditional acceptance of God is the privilege of all beings. To receive it, you do not have to trade your independent thought or your ability to choose experiences freely.

The concept of free will is often confused by religions and thus it is difficult to understand. How can it be that God allows us to choose any course of action without punishment? Surely He must punish us for our wrong choices? Many religions will tell us that we are blessed with the gift of free will, but we are not free to choose the "consequences" of it, which are often defined as "eternal punishments" that flow from our wrong choices.

How can this be free will? That is like saying to someone, "You have the choice to sit on this chair of mine, but if you do, I will shoot you." In reality there is not much choice in the matter. True free will necessarily requires that there are no "punishments" or eternal, negative consequences.

If we only make higher choices because we are rewarded for them, or we act only to avoid eternal punishments, then our actions are selfish and motivated by fear or greed. With such motivations, it is difficult to learn the power of unconditional love, God's love. If, however, there are no eternal punishments attached to our actions, and no eternal rewards are connected to our good deeds, then our higher choices can only be motivated out of unconditional love. This is a selfless motivation. This is the motivation inspired by God.

Like the concept of free will, we must be careful to preserve the gift of free thought. Many choose to believe certain things simply because an authority figure has endorsed them. Often they believe unconditionally in the written word, not recognizing that the words in the book were written by a person as frail, weak, and as prone to making mistakes as they are, despite their titles, designations or legends. Meanwhile, they are hesitant to put value in what they themselves think.

Practicing religion for many people often means an intellectual assent to the totality of their doctrines. Religious leaders love to learn the doctrines of their religion, studying each nuance to draw relationships between concepts that may or may not actually exist. As they reiterate to their believers these profound concepts that serve only to reinforce what has been taught to them by others, all delight in the apparent learning.

But take a person's beliefs and challenge them, force that person to acknowledge the weaknesses of their logic and reexamine everything he or she has previously taken for granted, and distress and anguish are sure to follow. For real thinking is difficult and does not provide us with the security many seem to crave.

We must not, indeed cannot, be afraid to apply logic and reason, in addition to intuition and feeling, to the religious beliefs we were taught as children or adults. If the doctrines are eternal truths, they will survive the scrutiny. If they do not endure, then they are no longer needed for our experience. Being open-minded and unafraid of utilizing the mental, intellectual and emotional processes that our Creator provided us will help us strip away the superstitions and false doctrines of life and man.

Religious doctrines throughout time have crumbled when they can no longer withstand the weight of contrary evidence and reason. We should not fear this process, but should welcome it. Rely not on that which others tell you, rather think for yourself. Challenge and test the perimeters of your beliefs and open the doors and windows that will allow new and different beliefs to enter. If you do, your mind and spirit will grow.

Remember that true spirituality does not come from being able to use words and logic better than the next to express and explain doctrine. In fact, such focus often steers us away from our spiritual core. True spirituality comes from realization: becoming love, not just exercising it. From becoming the divine Being we worship.

Brave is the person who does not readily accept the so-called popular faith. Thoughtful is the person who does not allow his or her belief to become mundane and careless. Open-minded is the person who constantly challenges all thought, including his own. Courageous is the person willing to consider the abandonment of previously-held beliefs in the light of new contradicting facts, intuition or revelation. And wise is the person who refuses to see life only through the colored glass of her own experience.

Seek these people, for it is they who will help you find the truth.

5.

Spiritual growth is an individual path.

Even when we feel uneasy about a particular spiritual practice or religious doctrine, or when something inside us tells us all is not right, or beliefs we are taught to hold sacred and have "faith in" strike us as wrong, we often continue to conform and allow religious organizations to have power over us because of our need for approval.

But as we have discussed, the fact is, over time, you can lose something important to your spiritual progression. As a member of such spiritual groups, you can lose the ability to think for yourself and dictate your own relationship with God. Individual spirituality threatens the stability of religious organizations and for this reason few religions embrace it. Unless a person's thoughts conform to the organization's doctrines, the individual's contributions are rarely valued and are often dismissed.

Be wary of organizations or people who ask you either explicitly or implicitly to believe their doctrines solely on the authority of the person or entity claiming responsibility for "being the voice of God." Often, such people or organizations focus more on the doctrines and theories that differentiate them from other organizations and that help them control their members, rather than on the principles for which the organization was founded in the first place.

All religions and churches have produced women and men of exalted character and spirit. Yet, despite this fact, some still believe that spirituality or divinity are the exclusive possessions of a single church or religion. You would be wise to cast a skeptical eye towards such religious organizations. By their very act of organizing, they often separate and divide, rather than bring people closer together. Too much hatred, persecution and violence in this world has been committed under the cloak of religion. Although religious organizations try to convince us that their acts of exclusion or punishment are really helping the sinner with "tough love," their actions always result in the same consequences for the individual – exclusion, a lack of love and acceptance, and a loss of self-worth.

If loving others means that you must exclude or punish them – it is better not to love in that way. In reality, exclusion is not love, it is punishment. It is hell and damnation. Exclusion ultimately prevents the unconditional love of all people – our divine objective. If you open your spiritual eyes you will see that the true and universal characteristics of God, qualities such as charity, compassion, and love, are demonstrated and taught by many different people, from all walks of life who represent many different religions, creeds and organizations.

As Albert Einstein once stated: "I cannot imagine a God who rewards and punishes the objects of His own creation, whose purposes are modeled after our own – a God, in short, who is a reflection of human frailty." Indeed, a controlling God of eternal rewards and punishments is a God that is jealous, vindictive and a mirror of our own fears and insecurities. It is not a God that I can any longer comprehend. It is certainly not a God that represents the highest ideals of love, compassion, experience and individual choice. This is the God that I believe in today. A God that honors the path of the individual, whatever that path might be, for it knows that the individual is merely a manifestation of Itself.

The real essence of God and divinity can only be found within oneself. Once we find it, we become empowered and independent. It is enough to place faith and belief, not in people who proclaim to be the representatives of God on Earth, but rather directly in our own relationship with God. It is enough to place faith in our own individual spiritual development, and learn to communicate directly with that entity responsible for our creation. As Jesus taught, the kingdom of heaven is within us.

We are not sinners, we are divine. The highest realization we can attain on this earth is the recognition of this divine heritage: that we already are what God is. Our spiritual task, then, is simply experiencing and demonstrating this divinity.

6.

Let your light so shine that others can see God in you.

If a person is deluded by a mirage for a period of time, and one day the mirage disappears, a change inevitably and irrevocably occurs. If the mirage reappears in the life of that person, he or she will not be so easily deluded again. Before the mirage first disappeared, the person understandably could not distinguish between reality and the deception of the mirage. But once the deception is revealed, once the mirage has been broken, if the person is true to herself and has the courage to accept the change, they will see the mirage but no longer will be deluded.

Seeing a mirage is like pursuing spiritual truth. Once understanding and spiritual learning occurs, there is no turning back. There is no return.

As you begin to open your spiritual eyes to see that truth and divinity ultimately lie only within you, you will begin to distinguish yourself spiritually from others. Your spirituality will no longer be simply a mirror of the beliefs of others, but, rather, will become a mirror of your own soul, your own divinity. As you begin to make such a transformation, you will begin to see everything in a new light.

Despite the greatness we give to some people and some teachings, the truth remains that, notwithstanding the source of their inspiration, everyone comes to us subject to their own experiences, prejudices, and beliefs. The experiences and beliefs of any person we have exalted are no better than ours, just different. The teachings of such individuals are useful because they provide a perspective on life that is different than our own. They are valuable, but only because they give our judgments perspective. They should never be accepted, however, as ultimate truth for all people, for in fact they only illuminate some truth for some people.

Ultimate truth lies not in the specific experience or beliefs of any one person, group, or religion. Rather, ultimate truth can only be approached by understanding and considering the sum of all belief, all experience, all life, and then pursuing that which touches your individual heart.

Do not allow yourself to become dependent on the teachings of others. If you are already dependent, free yourself and begin to explore your own individual spirituality. If you cannot live, learn, grow or succeed spiritually on your own, then there is a problem. I do not want to live upon the words and theories of others. If there is an existence beyond that obvious to my senses, like I believe there is, then I want to find it. If there is a soul in me that is not matter, if there is an all powerful force or God that affects me, I want to know it and become it. I do not wish to engage in the traditional struggles to prove specific dogmas or doctrines. Rather the glory of life, love and spirit to me is in realizing: being and becoming divine.

The true glory of our greatest leaders is not that they have thousands of loyal followers, but is found in their creation and inspiration of other great leaders. The true glory of a teacher is not found in the number of their students or in the amount of knowledge they convey, but rather is found in their enabling others to learn for themselves. The true glory of Jesus, like that of other spiritual teachers, is not found in simply following him, but rather is found in emulating and practicing his teachings and learning to love others as he did.

It is a divine truth that the moment we grow closest to God, is the moment we no longer need Her. For in this moment we, ourselves, act like God - we love like God, and every thought and every action we have is divine. We realize, in fact, we **are** God and God *is* us, and together we are **One**. The greatest glory and joy of God is when we, God's parts, recognize the divine heritage from which we are created and we manifest this divinity to others.

There is a story of a lioness who, while searching for food, came upon a flock of sheep. As she was about to attack one of them she went into labor, and gave birth to a baby cub. The labor was difficult and she died shortly thereafter. The young lion cub, knowing no better, immediately attached itself emotionally to one of the sheep.

This young cub was brought up in the flock of sheep, eating grass, and bleating like the other sheep. It never knew its true identity as a lion. One day another lion was preparing to attack the flock when he noticed that among it was a huge lion eating grass and bleating like the rest of the sheep. The flock saw the approaching lion and immediately took flight. Intrigued by the lion amongst the sheep, the approaching lion chased and stopped the lion-sheep to ask him about his abnormal behavior.

He told the lion-sheep that he was a lion, but the lion-sheep said no and began to bleat like a sheep. The stranger lion then took the lion-sheep to a nearby lake and asked him to look in the water at his reflection. He showed the lion-sheep how his appearance was similar to his own. The lion-sheep looked and acknowledged the resemblance. Then, the stranger lion roared and asked the lion-sheep to roar also. The lion-sheep tried and, with a little practice, was soon roaring like the stranger lion. Through his willingness to learn and discover new "facts" about his true essence, in no time at all the lion was a sheep no longer.

This analogy, of course, applies to our own lives. While we can learn a lot about God, spirit and ourselves from others, we must also learn not to be as sheep, following and emulating completely the thoughts and beliefs of others. We must find our own way. We must be our own persons, learning to focus on our strengths and develop our own, individual, divine attributes. We must think of ourselves as Gods, and learn to act and think as we believe God would. We are nothing less than God and thus we must learn God-like attributes.

But we cannot run before we walk.

Our personal spirituality is a progression of ideas, beliefs, and interactions with spirit that allow us to understand more deeply. This spiritual evolution occurs, like all progress, one step at a time. There seems to be essentially three stages of spiritual evolution. In the first we see God as a distant being who we fear and do not understand. We do not know when He will reward us or punish us and we only hope for His mercy.

With time and increased understanding, we enter the second stage where we feel more comfortable approaching God. We give Him omnipresence and omniscience so that He has the power to affect our lives. In this stage, we seek God's forgiveness and mercy and attribute to Him all that is good and divine. We hope to one day live with Him.

When learning about the true nature of God becomes our primary focus in life and we open our minds to understand and grow spiritually, we enter the final stage of spiritual evolution. In this stage we recognize God's hand and presence in all things – be it good or bad. We begin to understand and recognize that, in fact, we are God and She is us. In this final state of spiritual development we are content to love for sake of love, serve for the sake of service, and act in all things without hope of reward or fear of punishment. In this last stage, we are concerned not with the worship of or obedience to God, but rather with the realization of our own godliness.

This idea of acknowledging that we are God is not one we are commonly taught in our culture. On the contrary, if you look carefully you will see that many of the common perceptions of

God we are taught in fact incorporate more human traits than divine ones. For instance, we are often taught that God loves each and every one of us, but if we do not obey or worship Him we will be punished or condemned. This principle assumes that God needs or wants our worship and obedience. God wants our appreciation, not our worship or obedience. History is replete with examples of people who have killed to have people worship, serve and obey them. Obedience and worship are human demands, not divine ones. They are the projections of men who believe that an all-powerful God seeks and desires what they seek and desire.

God is much greater than that. God is above the vain desires of humans and is truly a parent in the grandest sense. She desires that we have free will with which to experience all things, and by doing so, learn to love and recognize the divinity within us. In Her infinite wisdom She allows us to stumble, fall, and fail without punishment, knowing that the punishment we will ultimately give ourselves is enough. She loves us unconditionally and inspires love within us. She sees the bigger picture, the all, and knows that through our experience we grow – whether our experience is **seemingly** good or bad, right or wrong. God does not worry about the moment, for She sees eternally. She is willing to tolerate the pain of today that we create, for She sees the glory of our tomorrow.

As you develop your divinity and as your spirit begins to grow, be careful about taking too much pride in your own spirituality or the path you have chosen to develop it. When you begin to believe that you are more spiritual than the next person, you travel not towards freedom but rather towards forging a stronger chain for your feet.

Pride of spirituality is probably worse than any other form of bondage. It is more binding than the bondage of the heart and soul that often comes from wealth, vanity or power. To believe that you are more pure than any other is perhaps the most damaging idea that can enter into the human heart or mind, as it carries eternal and divine implications. How are you more pure? The divinity in you comes from the same source as the divinity in any other. The God that is in you is the God in all. In all life, God is. We are all one and God is one with us.

Thus, true spirituality, true divinity, embraces all – from the lowest and vilest forms of our human existence, to the highest and most loving. True spirituality does not judge, but rather understands and encourages. True spirituality does not have place for persecution or intolerance, but rather warmly accepts difference. True spirituality is not proud; it is humble. True spirituality recognizes divinity in every man, woman and child, indeed in every living thing. True spirituality has the sole purpose of helping all humanity realize its divine nature.

Find your spirit, your divinity, the godliness that exists in you. Find your light so that you may pursue your divine purpose. And let that light so shine that others may see God in you and be inspired to pursue their own divine purpose.

Expectation

So far we have been discussing natural laws of commission, those things in life that we should be actively pursuing to bring happiness to our lives. However, the next topic of our discussion and part of the Law of Self Realization is a natural law of omission. That is to say, there is something that we need to learn to omit from our lives: expectation. According to the Law of Self Realization, to be truly happy, we must learn to let go of expectations.

Happiness = <u>Balance</u> – **_Expectation_** + <u>Purpose x Love</u>

Losing expectation is not something accomplished easily. Ultimately, it means that we must let go, stop making judgments, and stop trying to control everything. Losing expectation, however, does not mean ceasing to act proactively to create what it is we want. As we will learn in one of the sections that follow, an essential element to our self-realization is living a purposeful existence.

Rather, losing expectation means that we allow life to present us with new options and opportunities. It means not becoming so attached to a result that we lose sight of, or the chance to pursue, other opportunities or paths that may lead us to even greater heights than we are capable of imagining. As you will read in the following section, losing expectation is an essential element to restoring magic in our lives and allowing us to pioneer new paths in our sacred journey.

1.

Life is most lived when attachment to result is lost.

There is a story told of an old man and his boy who live on a farm. One day while riding out in the woods, they came upon a dozen wild horses that they managed to round up and bring back to their farm. When they heard the news, all of the townspeople said to the old man what a good thing it was that he and his boy found these wild horses. The old man, however, just shrugged his shoulders and said, "maybe it is, maybe it is not – it is too early to tell."

Several weeks later there was a storm. During the night, the horses became spooked and knocked down the farmer's fence and destroyed part of his barn. In an attempt to try and stop the wild horses from running away, the farmer's son broke his leg. Upon hearing the news, the townspeople said to the old man, what a bad thing finding the wild horses was after all, as it led to the breaking of his son's leg. The old man, however, just shrugged his shoulders and said, "maybe it is, maybe it is not – it is too early to tell."

Another month passed and war broke out between neighboring villages. All of the available young men who were healthy were called to war. Because of his broken leg, however, the farmer's son could not go and fight. The villagers again approached the old man, this time stating to the farmer what a good thing it was that he found the wild horses, because it led to the breaking of his son's leg. With a broken leg, he could not go to war and risk being killed. The old man, however, just shrugged his shoulders and said, "maybe it is, maybe it is not – it is too early to tell."

Sure enough, a week later a fire broke out in the farmer's barn while he was away. The son was unable to do anything because of his broken leg. The barn burned to the ground and many of the animals ran away. The villagers again went to the old man, this time stating that it was a bad thing after all that he first found the wild horses, for if the son's leg had not been broken, he could have saved the barn from burning. Again the old man just shrugged his shoulders and said, "maybe it is, maybe it is not – it is too early to tell."

You can see the point of this story. It is a good example of the foolishness behind judgment. Until all of the consequences of an action are known, we cannot make a judgment about whether an event is good or bad. And if we cannot make such a judgment, then how can we have expectation in a particular result? Perhaps the result we intend will be less beneficial to us than the result that will occur if our course is altered in the face of an intervening event or change.

It is difficult to learn to live life without expectation or attachment to anticipated results. It is difficult because we are trained from a very early age to seek results and to do what it takes to succeed. Having goals and taking steps to achieve the results we want, however, is fine. The trick is to detach ourselves from the anticipated result once we have set our intention into motion. The teacher Dennis Wholey once commented: "happy people plan actions, they don't plan results." We cannot be so wedded to anticipated results that we fear or reject other alternatives that life offers. The events in our lives that we believe, at the moment, are the most disastrous, can often be the ones that ultimately bring us the most achievement and satisfaction. How many times in your own life has something that you initially thought would be negative, in fact turned out to be something quite positive?

Every day we must practice ridding ourselves of emotional attachment to results. You can and should prepare yourself for what it is you want to achieve and accomplish. But despite all of your preparation and desire to achieve, you still may not get the results you want. Do not fear, and do not be concerned. Let life lead you where it may. Resist the temptation of becoming judgmental of your circumstances. You do not know where they are ultimately taking you.

You can and should act to change things in your life that you do not like or that you know do not contribute to your happiness. You should in all cases follow the promptings of your heart. But be careful not to depend emotionally on the anticipated results of your actions. For if you do not get those results, misery will surely follow. Rather, prepare yourself, follow your heart, act in a way you know is right for you, and then see where life takes you. Believe that the best things will result for you in all situations over the long term.

Life is much easier and you will be much happier when you

free yourself from the chains of expectations. You must learn to give up attachment and expectation if you ultimately want to rid your life of misery. Misery comes only from attachment. When we become attached to things or results, we lose our freedom.

If you read in the paper of a man who loses a beautiful painting because of a fire, how much misery do you feel? Probably not much. However, if it is your painting that is lost, how do you feel? Totally miserable, probably. Although the painting in both cases may have been the same, our feeling of misery usually only comes from the destruction of the one to which we are attached.

For many people, misery comes with the sense of possession. To be truly happy, we must learn to lose this sense of possession. Everything in our life we are lucky enough to experience is a blessing, not a possession. We are lucky to have an experience with any thing or person, no matter how long we are lucky enough to have the experience. Some believe that we must give up physical possessions to reach freedom from misery. But a person who gives up his car, house, clothes, and jewelry has not necessarily lost his attachment. He may have simply replaced his attachment to those riches with a new attachment, like one for religion or for abstinence. You could be the richest woman in the world and have no attachments, while another could give up all worldly possessions but still be very much attached.

Non-attachment does not mean getting rid of physical possessions. Getting rid of attachment is a process of the mind. The link that forms the "mine" of our existence is within, not without. If we rid ourselves of this link, then we become unattached and we rid ourselves of misery.

2.

All of these things shall give thee experience.

The loss of expectation in our lives should realign much of our focus that is spent on the future back to the present moment. For once expectation is lost, the present moment becomes the most important object of our focus. As we lose expectation and begin to focus on the present circumstances in our lives, it is important to remember that all things teach us and allow us to grow. All things give us experience.

Our task in life, quite simply, is to gain experience and from these experiences to learn to make choices that reflect who we really are. Nothing more, nothing less. But do not underestimate the magnificence or the magnitude of this task. It encompasses all life, all emotions, and all experience. It assumes both an outward journey through circumstance and an inward journey through feeling. It assumes an outward interaction with others, and introspection into our own minds and souls. It incorporates good and evil, love and hate, fear and security.

The journey of our soul encompasses all experience. It has to, for experience is the only way the soul can realize its full potential and glory. The soul cannot understand and embrace love until it knows what it is like to not love. The soul cannot choose and appreciate good, until it knows what evil is and has felt its effects. The soul cannot experience true happiness and security, until it can contrast those feelings with the experience of fear. All experience is necessary for our progression.

For this reason we should appreciate and bless adversity in our lives and learn not to judge ourselves for the mistakes we believe we make or the contradictions in our being. It is not always **being** what we want to be that helps us become what we want to be. Rather, it is adversity and contrary experience that often causes our most significant growth.

You cannot condemn that which you believe does not represent the divine either in yourself or in others, for without it you would not recognize the divine. If all you ever ate since the day you were born were sweet things, you would not appreciate or recognize sweet, because you would have nothing with which to contrast it. To truly appreciate sweetness you must experience bitterness. Therefore, when you come upon a difficult circumstance in the harmony of your life, offer special thanks for the circumstance and love the deliverer. By offering their striking contrast, they will make your general experience and harmony that much sweeter.

To fully understand and appreciate anything, we must be exposed to its opposite. Do not despise, therefore, that which is opposite of the values or experiences you embrace. Be thankful for them, for they permit you to realize and appreciate your full potential. Likewise, in your quest for happiness, remember that ***pleasure*** can never be enduring, nor should we want it to be. The force and experience of pleasure would cease to exist if we never had other experiences against which we could compare it. Ultimately, our true purpose must be to seek the knowledge and wisdom that comes from experience.

Our pursuit of knowledge and experience cannot fail. We only feel failure when we replace the quest for knowledge and experience with the desire for pleasure. Pleasure is never enduring. What we must do to grow in wisdom is to consider both pleasure and pain as great teachers, for we learn from both. While we often try to avoid experiences of pain, misery and discomfort, they bring us greater knowledge and wisdom than we would otherwise have without them. From adversity and pain spring fortitude, courage, and wisdom.

We must learn to be like an eagle that uses wind to soar higher. From the winds of our experience and adversity we, too, soar higher. Ultimately, it is upon a perch at the top of the highest mountain that we see the splendor and grandeur of life. It is here we sit with God.

The ultimate purpose in life is for us to know ourselves as divine, as God. To do this, we must gain experience. All experience, both good and bad, leads us to this divine awareness. The good experiences we have help us to feel the glory of God and lead us to that which is divine. The perceived negative experiences we have help us to learn what we are not, and also lead us to that which is divine. Thus, both negative and positive experiences are essential to our manifestation of life.

Good experiences that allow us to feel the glory of God can only be appreciated and distinguished when they are contrasted with their opposite experiences. Both are necessary and essential to our spiritual experience. The speed at which we consciously mature, however, is dependent upon the types of experiences we choose to repeat in our lives.

3.

To *be* or not to *be* are equal parts of *being*.

Once we lose expectation and we begin to understand that everything in life is designed to give us experience, we can begin to make the most important decision of our lives: who and what do we want to be. This is not a question of whether we want to be a doctor, a teacher, or an artist, but rather it is a question of what do we want to do, and what can we do, to manifest ourselves as the highest vision we have of ourselves.

Since the beginning of time mystics, religionists, philosophers, and many others have asked these kinds of questions. They are usually framed as questions about the meaning or purpose of life. The answer to the question about our reason for being is this: to experience who we are and who we choose to be.

In the beginning there was nothing else other than universal energy or spirit (which I will call God). This God knew only one thing: that there was nothing else other than itself. Consequently, without anything else against which to compare itself, God could not know itself. Yet God, to be complete, wanted to know itself through the experience of being something that could relate to itself.

God must have reasoned that if it divided itself into parts smaller than the whole, each part, when connecting with the whole, would be able to feel the magnificence of the whole, for it would be able to experience the individual part and its absence from the whole. So, God divided itself, its energy, into many things, and by doing so created the experience of relativity: the relationship of a part to the whole.

This was the greatest gift that God ever did for itself and for us. By dividing itself into many individual parts and creating this relationship to the whole, God created the ability to not only know itself, but also to allow its parts to know and feel their relationship to the whole, to appreciate the grandeur of the whole.

Thus, God is the author of all: good and bad, love and fear, happiness and unhappiness – everything. What we perceive as the negative side of life is absolutely necessary as a part of the whole. Without the negative, we could never put the positive into perspective, we could never truly enjoy it. In fact, there would be no positive. This law of opposites, the division of the whole into opposing and separate parts, underlies all experience. This polarity in life allows us to fully experience godliness, or the whole.

Often people focus on the negative and ask how God can allow what we view as the negative aspects of life to exist. The real question we should ask, however, is how could God have done anything different? If we did not have negative experience, we could never have known or appreciated positive experience. To feel joy you must know what it is to be sad – then you understand the value of joy and happiness. Likewise, to experience pure love and acceptance, you must know what it is to be unaccepted, to be unloved. In the moment that fear, rejection and the absence of love are created, love becomes a thing that can be experienced and appreciated fully.

When something happens that you perceive as negative, rather than focus on its negativity, focus on that which the negative allows you to experience more fully. When someone rejects you or stops loving you, use this moment to focus on the fact that you now know better what it is to love more completely. Approach the moment as a teacher of the value of unconditional love and all that is good in your life.

Each and every day of your life, in fact, each and every moment of your life, beginning with right now, you have the opportunity to choose who it is you are, and how you will manifest yourself to others. In every circumstance you have a choice of how you will perceive the events, a choice of how you will react to them, and a choice of whether you will learn anything from them. You may feel that much of your reaction to life's events is involuntary and for many it may be. But the truth of the matter is that, even if you do not **consciously** choose your reactions, perceptions, and representations, you **unconsciously** choose them. After years and years of habit and unconscious learning, we learn to act unconsciously.

The first step towards change is awareness: understanding that our life experience is largely a matter of perception, and this perception can be altered. The second step is learning to suspend our judgment of anything as either good or bad, and beginning to simply accept things as they really are: simply distinct and different aspects of the whole. Only one decision really matters relating to our physical existence and experience: which thoughts and actions do we, and will we, choose to represent who we are? Every moment of every day we are all making this decision, only many of us make it unconsciously. God does not care what choices we make, for all choices provide God with the experience of relationship to itself. So we are left, as individual manifestations of God, to decide what kind of individual experience we will have. We cannot make a wrong decision, for all choices bring experience, understanding and growth.

It is important to learn that we are individual, physical manifestations of God. When we know this, we become empowered to accept and love ourselves regardless of the choices we have made in the past. When we finally understand our divine heritage, we become free to choose today, and forever more, those actions, reactions and perceptions that represent the highest vision we have of ourselves. And we become free to focus our attention on our higher purpose.

Purpose

You will remember from our earlier discussion the Law of Self Realization:

Happiness = <u>Balance – Expectation + **Purpose** x Love</u>

True and lasting happiness is created when we are balanced in body, mind and spirit; when we lose expectation or attachment to specific results; when we have a purpose to which our life is directed; and when everything we do is motivated by and centered in love. In the creation of happiness, these elements are not chronological steps to be applied in order, but rather they are elements of our lives that should command our awareness, focus and attention. So, for example, one should not hold off developing their purpose until he or she is balanced. Nor should someone refrain from acting out of love at all times until he or she has learned to lose expectation. Rather, each of the elements of this formula should be thought of and acted upon on a daily basis in order to establish happiness in our lives as a permanent resident.

The next topic of our discussion is purpose. Like all the elements in our formula, without Purpose the formula fails and happiness will remain somewhat elusive. With it, our lives become enriched, focused, and rewarding and we become closer to filling our lives with the happiness and peace we so desperately seek.

1.

The balance of body, mind and spirit facilitates the focus of the soul on purpose.

It can take an entire lifetime, or perhaps many lifetimes, to achieve the proper balance of body, mind and soul. It is not achieved overnight, but that should not be surprising considering our bad habits are usually created over many years. But once we become aware of the importance of balance, and we begin to spend a part of every day focusing on and developing our mind, body and spirit, a funny thing begins to happen. We will begin to think and feel we have a purpose beyond mere pleasure distractions, beyond our mere existence.

It is a natural thing for every person to feel as though they have a purpose or reason for being. But for many people struggling to find happiness through pleasure distractions, a sense of purpose is never realized and sometimes never even recognized. For some, life is a continual focus on events, from birth to adolescence, to adulthood, and in adulthood from job to job and acquisition to acquisition. Such distractions never satisfy the soul, however, and once the "newness" of the present job, acquisition or relationship has gone away, some new stimulus must be found.

This struggle breeds a sense of impatience and a "searching" for something that never seems to be attained. Often those caught in this struggle can explain the symptoms, such as boredom, lack of present-moment focus, un-fulfilling relationships and jobs, etc., but they cannot explain why they feel the way they do or how to overcome such feelings. The reason for these feelings, however, is quite simple: they arise whenever we have no sense of purpose, no reason for being that motivates our choices.

To the person who sees beyond pleasure distractions, who cares enough to open their awareness to the proper development of body, mind and spirit, and who diligently works each day to develop these parts of themselves, comes a focused sense of purpose and being. And, oh, how powerful this focus can be!

Many of us may recall as children taking a magnifying glass outside and focusing the rays of the sun through the magnifying glass to create an intense beam of light capable of burning almost anything. When we properly balance our body, mind and spirit, we create a vehicle much like the magnifying glass; we become able to focus the energy and spirit of life through ourselves to create an intense beam that is capable of enormous achievement. I like to call this phenomenon the "focus of being."

Even those that are not particularly balanced in life, but who concentrate their energies into a single area can create an intense focus of being that is capable of substantial achievement. The difference between the focus of one who is balanced and one who is not, however, is usually found in the object of their focus:

one who is balanced in body, mind, and spirit will more often than not choose an area of focus that is borne out of, and motivated by, love rather than fear.

Focus of being is essential to our well-being and happiness. It is like the rudder of a prized racing yacht that helps steer the racing vessel quickly and efficiently to its desired destination. Without the rudder, the yacht may be capable of moving quickly, but it will have difficulty going anywhere or staying on course. Likewise, without a sense of purpose we may be capable of great things, but we will have difficulty achieving them.

2.

Purpose of being can never be attained without the willingness to define and stand for what you believe.

How confidently do you stand for your principles? How secure are you in your beliefs and values? How willing are you for the whole world to see and hear what you believe? Think about these questions very seriously and be honest with your self-evaluation. Unless you can confidently proclaim to the world who you are and what you stand for, you either do not know who you are or you are not happy with yourself.

You must learn to become confident in your beliefs. You can achieve this by closely examining everything you think you believe and determining whether or not these beliefs really represent you, or whether they are simply vestiges from your past: beliefs handed down from parents, friends and organizations, that you have never completely accepted.

If any of your beliefs are the latter, it is time to do a little house cleaning. You owe it to yourself and to your happiness to determine who you are and what you stand for. And you must be honest. The beliefs and values you hold dear must be those that you truly believe in. They cannot be the beliefs that anyone else in your life thinks you should have. If your beliefs do not truly represent you, then you will not be willing to stand up and proclaim them to others. You will not be willing to defend them, nor will you be willing to share them.

Beliefs and values that you hold which do not truly represent you will strip you of self-worth and confidence. They will confuse and distract you from your sense of purpose and will become obstacles in the achievement of your greatest dreams. Ultimately, they will become like a cancer, killing your enthusiasm and your passion.

Take it upon yourself to discard those beliefs and values that you know do not represent you. Embrace and employ those values in your life that do represent who you are or what you want to become. And for those that you are unsure, take the time to explore your beliefs and values. Learn about them and test them, so you can decide whether or not they represent the grandest vision you have of yourself.

Your beliefs must represent you; they cannot represent that which someone else is telling you to believe. Only you can decide who you are and what you stand for. It is never too late to emerge from the shadows of the beliefs of others and begin to fashion your own identity – one that you can proudly proclaim to be your own. Once you do, you will be well on your way to realizing your purpose and becoming truly happy.

3.

Intention never matures into Purpose without realization through action.

Unfortunately in life there is sometimes a disconnection between what a person is and what a person perceives themselves to be. This misperception can go either way. For some, everyone's opinion of them may be good and positive, but the perception they have of themself is negative. For such people, lack of self-esteem is an obstacle that must be overcome. For others, despite the fact that others may view them in a negative light, they see themselves as being quite positive. Often this discrepancy is caused by a lack of connection between thought and action.

In general, other people's opinion of us should not matter. But opinion can be instrumental to our own growth and development, especially when we begin to see patterns of our own behavior that we do not like. For example, if everyone we meet forms the same negative opinion of us, then it is relatively easy to conclude that we may indeed have an issue, even if it is simply an unintended image that we project. In such instances, it is perhaps wise to question what it is we may be doing that is communicating this perception, whether we believe it is accurate or not. It would also be wise to question whether or not we are converting our positive thoughts (seen by ourselves) into positive action (seen by others).

A person may have the grandest feelings and intentions towards others, but until those intentions are given life through action, they remain nothing more than intentions. And as we have all heard, the road to hell is paved with good intentions. While positive thoughts are the seeds from which positive actions follow, too often these thoughts never materialize into actions. One can have every thought of love and charity, but unless one does charitable and loving things as a result of those thoughts, one is robbed of the experience of love and charity.

Life is about experience and realizing our divine potential. This cannot be accomplished by thought alone; action is required. Once action or change is initiated, we may experience some negative responses, as it seems the universe likes to test our commitment to the action we have initiated. But positive thoughts and responses from others are also generated to support that positive intention and action. With these positive reactions come increased confidence and a sense of accomplishment, which in turn usually produce more of the behavior that gives rise to these reactions in the first place.

You may have heard the phrase "one good turn leads to another." Positive thoughts that are converted into action generate feelings and consequences that inevitably lead to more positive thoughts and actions. This process, in effect, becomes a positive cycle I call a "vertical updraft." This cycle goes ever upward in a spiraling pathway that ultimately leads to the full realization of our being. The catalyst for such updrafts is always action.

Action takes our good intentions and converts them into purpose. And purpose helps fill our souls with everlasting happiness and peace.

4.

The greatest purpose of all is that which empowers and enriches the lives of others.

A story is told how God once appeared and took unto himself a home on earth. Man soon discovered that God was here, and went to visit God in person, rather than do so in prayer. Man knocked on the door, and a voice answered from inside.

"Who is it?" the voice asked. "It is I, Man."

"What do you seek, Man?" the voice asked.

"I seek to speak with God and tell him of my desires," Man said. The door did not open, and there was silence. A second time Man knocked on the door.

"Who is it?" the voice asked. "It is I, Man."

"What do you seek, Man?" the voice asked.

"I seek to speak with God and tell him of my needs." Once again the door did not open. Man went a third time to the door.

"Who is it?" the voice asked. "It is your servant, Man."

"What do you seek, Man?" the voice asked.

"I seek to speak with God and find with Her ways to share my love for all mankind." Without a further moment's hesitation, the doors opened and Man was welcomed inside.

There is no singular purpose that is or should be the same for everyone. Only you, as an individual, can determine a path of purpose that is right for you. Every person has unique talents and gifts, and a wealth of individual experience. These talents and experiences help define who and what you are, and are the vehicles through which you can touch the lives of others.

The greatest aspect of our individuality is that we all have the ability to positively affect different people. Where I may have no positive affect on a certain person, you may change their life forever. Likewise, where your experiences and gifts may not touch the soul of an individual, perhaps mine will. This is the power and glory of our uniqueness and individuality.

This individuality is what brings glory and completion to the whole. It is through the collective experience of purpose, that is the combination of my purpose with your purpose and the purpose of others, that we are able to positively affect all people. No part is excluded and no individual is left out. This is why we all have so much to contribute, for we all form a part of the whole and can positively affect the whole. We do so by positively affecting the individual parts of the whole.

Do not, therefore, underestimate your purpose or that which you feel you can contribute to the world. Neither underestimate the purpose of any other person. For although you or I may only ever touch the life of one person, that person may go on to touch the lives of thousands. We hear little of the individuals who, in following their hearts, were responsible for inspiring and teaching individuals like Jesus, Mohammed, Buddha, Ghandi, and Mother Theresa. Yet these individuals all had their own teachers who helped influence their choices to become who they were. Are the consequences of their individual efforts, even though they may have only affected a single person, any less than those of the great individuals they helped develop?

Actions that further the development of who we really are and what we want to become are like tiny seeds that are strewn across the land as we walk. Certainly some may simply perish for lack of nourishment, but many will fall into cracks between rocks where they will grow, and many will fall into fertile soil that, with time, will allow them to grow and bloom in full. Still others will be carried by the wind to take root in fertile soil elsewhere. We likely will never see the full effects of our actions of purpose, but our failure to see the effects will never diminish their actual impact for change.

In a very simple way, the sum of your purposeful actions need amount to nothing more than making the world and the surroundings in which you live a better place because you are in it. If nothing else, you have the opportunity to positively affect everyone with whom you have contact. If you can do this, you have accomplished much.

The only judgments you should make of your actions and your purpose, is whether or not they enrich and empower the lives of others and whether they are inspired out of your love. To teach people of their divine spirit and of the fact that they are divinely loved and accepted regardless of what they do is one of the greatest acts of purpose possible, for spirit is the one common element of all lives. A person who is strong spiritually will be strong in every other respect. The most powerful people this world has ever known are those that have helped others find their spirit.

But remember not to seek praise or rewards for your actions. Learn, instead, to do your greatest work silently. Some of the greatest individuals our existence has ever produced have passed away unknown. The world knows nothing of these great men and women that have lived, for their lives and works have passed silently. Their actions, however, and their thoughts and ideas ultimately found expression in the Buddhas and Christs that we know.

Find your purpose and pursue it with all of your heart, might, mind and soul. Do not judge the results of your efforts for you will likely not see the ultimate and grand effects of your works. Know only that when you act out of love, with no expectation of return, you have the ability to change the world.

Love

From where, from when, to what,
ageless minds wonder why,
how often do we pursue,
questions that expose the lie?

There are those who tell us not to question
many more that, alone, do not wonder,
to these the movie is simply viewed,
their involvement put asunder,

> *but in special moments and places,*
> *if you ask and listen God will whisper,*
> *sacred passages to her spirit and to your soul,*
> *that you and all can enter,*
>
> *inside you will see, feel, and learn,*
> *that true love begins first with yourself,*
> *and in the end requires no return.*
> Austin Vickers

Love is everything; it is our universe and our atmosphere. It is our breath. The very essence of our life was created by love and is sustained by love. Love forms the basis for every genuine moment of our lives: our birth, our death, our sexuality and sensuality, our passion, our truth, our suffering, our happiness, our living and our dying. All of these are constructed out of and by love. Everything else is just a distraction. Our attention and our awareness should always be on getting past the distractions – to love, which is the very essence of life.

Love is, and should be, the very context by which you experience life.

Unfortunately, in our society, we seem to over-value power, money, and success. Little value, it seems, is given to those who have successfully learned to love. But do not be dismayed by the short-term praise that is heaped upon those that are successful in attaining worldly possessions or position. Their glory is but for a short time.

If you do nothing in this life other than learn to love unconditionally, your peace shall be sublime and your glory shall be eternal. While praise and appreciation for the person who has truly learned how to love may be limited to a much smaller audience, the depth of that appreciation among the few that recognize the value of love will greatly outweigh any temporary or superficial attention or joy that can come from having substantial amounts of worldly power, money or success.

The choice in life is really quite simple: do you wish to live and survive upon the approval of others, or do you wish to live your life according to the dictates of your own heart? Should you choose the former, be prepared for a life of insecurity and fleeting affections. Should you choose the latter, real happiness and peace will be your reward.

This is not to say that individuals who enjoy worldly possessions, power, or money are necessarily selfish, unloving, or do not have their focus on divine principles. You and I cannot judge the intent of a person's heart. It may be that from their ability to be selfless and their focus on unconditional love, they have been fortunate enough to also derive great success and worldly position. My counsel to you is simply that the intent of your heart and the aspiration of your life should be to truly understand and practice unconditional love. Nothing more, nothing less.

You will notice in the Law of Self Realization,

Happiness = Balance – Expectation + Purpose x **Love**

that everything is multiplied by love. In my opinion there are two aspects of love worthy of our distinction. One is the love that we show towards others. The other is the love that we need to have for ourselves. No discussion about love is complete, in my opinion, without a discussion of both kinds of love. Each is essential to a full and complete manifestation of the other. Without love of self, one cannot truly love another. When we do not or cannot show love towards others, it is likely we have no love for ourselves.

Before we address the subjects of love of self and others, however, it is important to discuss and understand what love is. It is also important in our development as loving beings that we understand what love is not. Only then can we begin the process of learning to love ourselves, and following that, loving others.

It is extremely difficult to explain what love is. It is much easier to see it, understand when we see it, and feel our reaction to it when we are in love's presence. It is easy to recognize when people act in a loving way and easy to see when our own loving feelings have been stirred. But we would do well to make it a priority to learn what love is. For most, our definitions of love, and more importantly our exhibitions of love, are emulations of those that we have seen or heard from others. More often than not, these examples better inform us of what love is not, rather than what love is.

Our existence begins in love. From the day we are born we seek, consciously or unconsciously, love's essence: unconditional love and acceptance. We seek for others to appreciate and value who we are. The problem many of us have, however, is that almost immediately from the day we were born, this unconditional love we seek is replaced with conditional acceptance. Whereas we wanted parents and friends to accept us despite our faults and weaknesses, we received acceptance more often than not only when we conformed to their expectations.

In short, we were and are given qualified acceptance based on "good behavior." We are rewarded for our good deeds and we are punished for our bad deeds. This cycle of reward and punishment is emphasized on a daily basis in our lives. It teaches us that we are only deserving of love when we act appropriately to receive it. How then can we expect it be ours continually? Love, treated like a reward, can never be what it truly is – the unconditional privilege of all.

Love is your birthright. The very essence of your being is love and it is not conditioned upon how you act. You are love despite your weaknesses, despite your perceived "failures." You have a right to unconditional beauty, compassion, kindness, understanding, and forgiveness. Your access to this unconditional love is never denied, you only choose at times to block it.

You have chosen at some point in your life to accept blocks that impede the flow of real love, either consciously or subconsciously. Because you put them there, the blocks in front of love can be removed only when you decide to remove them. No one else can do it for you. The key to removing these blocks is awareness. Awareness of what the blocks are, and why and when we put them in front of love, and awareness of how to remove such blocks.

The purpose of this section is to teach you this awareness. To teach you the truth about love.

1.

The truth about love is that love is our truth.

Often people think of love as a thing, an object, something that is to be acquired. We "look for love" in relationships, we sometimes believe people "do not give us enough love," and we wonder why this thing called love is absent from our lives. But love is not an object or a thing. It is something we do. We either love or we do not love. Love innately requires action. It is not love when we simply have an intention. Love requires that we *do* something. Active participation is a necessary element of love. Without action love is not love, it is a nice thought.

It is easy to see love in action. Things like service, passion, trust, respect, dignity, sincerity, kindness, patience and fairness are manifestations of the action that comprises love. Conversely, the opposite of these traits – disservice, apathy, disrespect, distrust, selfishness, impatience, meanness, degradation and unfairness - are manifestations of the absence of the action that love requires.

Thus, love is behavior. It is opening your ears to hear the pain of another. It is opening your eyes to the beauty of the world. It is feeling the touch of another human being. It is being aware of the beauty that exists all around you right now. It is opening your mind to learn. It is opening your heart to others and allowing yourself to love and be loved.

Love is letting go of judgment, attachment to results, expectations and fear. Love, in fact, is simply letting go. Like the tenets espoused by the Serenity Prayer, love is the serenity to accept things you cannot change; love is the courage to change the things you can; and love is the wisdom to know the difference.

But love is more. Love is that which inspires creativity, initiative and enthusiasm within us. Love is gratitude and appreciation. Love is that which brings us peace. Love is that which allows us to grow and evolve. Love is that which brings mystery and magic to our lives and amplifies our happiness.

Love neither exists in the past nor in the future. Love exists only in the present. Judgment exists in the past and the future. So does fear. When we find our minds immersed in thoughts about the past or the future, it is usually about fear or judgment that we are really thinking. We fantasize about the future and we replay our past choices. But love is content to patiently wait in the present. We often hurry backwards or forwards hoping to find love, but we move too quickly over the present where love resides and so we often miss it.

Take the time to focus on the present and you will find love. Being present moment focused brings love alive. This does not mean living **for** the moment. Living **for** the moment ignores tomorrow and can deprive us of tomorrow's gifts. Rather being present moment focused means we live **in** the moment. Living **in** the moment is different than living **for** the moment. Living in the moment acknowledges and considers tomorrow, but appreciates today.

Love is real and, thus, exists in this moment. Love does not exist in the imagined past or the speculative future. Love can learn the lessons from yesterday and anticipate tomorrow's dreams, but love does not dwell in the future or the past for it knows that tomorrow's dreams may never arrive and yesterday's lessons are only important for today.

Love has no bounds. It is timeless, borderless, vast, open and free. It has been compared to space, for like space, it is endless and beyond the full comprehension of man. Like space, it cannot be filled, it cannot be destroyed, and we cannot make it go away. We can fill space with objects that block our view of space but it is always there. When we search deep enough into the objects themselves, we once again find space. Love is the same. It is always there. We may block it and distract ourselves from its presence, but love never goes away, only we do. Despite the objects we throw at love, despite our attempts to destroy it, we cannot. Like space, love is a constant that is not affected by objects.

Love provides us with a chance to see eternity. It is the very essence of peace, happiness and satisfaction. Indeed, it is the inspiration behind these things. When we experience peace, happiness or satisfaction, we are enveloping ourselves for that brief moment in the essence of love. We are fulfilled by and filled with love in such moments. When we desire and the desire is fulfilled, the moment of satisfaction is the moment that love reigns freely and is allowed to envelop our very being. We often do not allow such moments to last and our egos and insecurities quickly return us to new desires. But the moment of fulfillment is when we come face to face with love and there is nothing in between it and us.

When I think of love I cannot help but think of it like I do the sun. It's rays shine on indefinitely, constantly, filling the vast expanse of the universe with its warmth and comfort. We cannot stop the sun from shining, we can only hide from it. We can block it, or put clouds or buildings in front of it. We can ignore it, avoid it, and shun it, but always it shines and warms us if we return to its embrace. So it is with love.

We may try to run from love, or we may deny it, but love is always there when we return. Like the rays of the sun through the clouds, eventually the rays of love shine on our hearts despite our attempts to hide from it. By its presence, our life is filled with light and comfort. Love is our constant companion. Love is that which exists around us always, it is that which fills our hearts and souls.

Love is our essence and when we recognize this, and when we allow it to shine within and from us, we become consumed in love's fire.

2.

The love we experience is directly proportionate to the degree in which we choose to see, and allow, love into our lives.

As cliché as it may sound, love is our only, and ultimate, reality. It is the clearest definition and experience of God there is. In love, we find God. When we love unconditionally we demonstrate our own godliness. Once you recognize the divine truth that love is all there is, you can more easily grasp the fact that loving is our only purpose in life. Unconditional love ultimately has been the goal of every spiritual master that has ever lived. Their lives are nothing more than examples of the behavior and characteristics of love. In every thought, every action, every moment of their lives, love was their choice, not fear.

To fill our lives with love, we must overcome its eternal opposite – fear. Fear is that which makes our love conditional. Fear is that which makes us forget the purpose of our lives. Fear is that which makes us focus on the self, rather than on the object of our love. Every action in life can be analyzed at its core as being motivated by fear or love.

Love is the opposite of fear in that it is an act of selflessness, not selfishness. Love gives no thought to the self, like fear does, but rather thinks more of the beneficiary of the act. Love always has the best interest of others in mind. Love requires no gratitude the way fear does, because it is given unconditionally without an expectation of a return. Love also does not concern itself with the loss of appreciation like fear does, because love is not insecure like fear is.

Each day we are presented with countless opportunities to act – either out of love or out of fear. As we have previously discussed, there are no automatic actions or reactions, only ones we choose not to consciously consider. If we seemingly act or react automatically in any situation or to any person or thing, it is only because we have failed to consciously choose our action or reaction to the situation, person or thing. Love, too, is a choice. It is a choice to open one's heart to self and to others. It is a decision one can make from one day to the next. Love does not simply happen, it is a conscious decision to allow. The love we experience and see in the world is directly proportionate to the degree in which we **choose** to see love in the world.

Every situation and every circumstance presents an opportunity for love or fear. Our view of the world is simply the conscious or subconscious choice of whether we will recognize love or fear. To the extent we wish, in every circumstance, situation, or relationship we can make the choice to love. If we follow that choice with supportive action, our love will grow, develop, widen, sustain itself, and reach farther into our collective souls than we might ever have imagined was possible.

Developing an aptitude for love and loving is no different than any other habit or skill we decide to develop. First, we must have the desire to acquire or develop the skill. Second, we must begin to acquire the knowledge and facts about the skill, so that we can learn how it is developed. Finally, we must practice the skill by beginning to consciously exercise it until it becomes a habit or an automatic response.

If I exercise my body on a daily basis, then I will become physically stronger, faster and more developed. If I study a subject every day I will become trained in that subject and eventually I will become an expert on it. The same is true for love. It is an acquired skill. It requires desire, awareness, knowledge, and practice until the skill becomes habitual. If we spent even a fraction of the time developing our capacity to love and be loved as we do getting an education, playing a sport or a musical instrument, or working at our jobs, we would drastically and significantly impact our lives. Love, you see, is powerful and transforming.

No one who has developed a great capacity to love will tell you it is easy. Learning to love and be loved is perhaps one of the hardest things we can do, for great teachers of love are not abundant. We do not find courses in schools or universities that teach us about love. Those that are closest to us, like parents, teachers and friends, are usually so busy dealing with their own issues that they, too, do not provide us with good examples of how to love. So, we have to take on the responsibility ourselves. We have to learn from those that speak of love. We have to practice the principles they teach to see if they work for us. And we have to spend the time and effort every day to learn the art of loving. We cannot escape the demands that loving and being loved require. But once we learn to love, neither will we be able to escape love's rewards.

This work, the work of love, is often not pursued because of the alternatives offered by our culture that placate many of us, and that are seductively attractive. Modern culture presents a wide variety of stimuli and what I like to call "pleasure distractions" that provide us with every incentive not to undergo the hard work of love. Pleasure distractions are easily pursued, but their rewards are never enduring: the hunger of the soul quickly returns. True and everlasting love, on the other hand, is only acquired through patience, work, desire and dedication. But once achieved, the rewards of love continue indefinitely, satisfying the hunger of our soul.

When we first begin to open our hearts and explore inside, we often find a lot of grief and sorrow. The heart is the home of buried feelings and pain and, when we begin to open the heart in our search for love, we are confronted with these things. The experience of this pain and sorrow, however, is that which allows us to love more fully, for it offers us a striking contrast with which we can then appreciate love. Be confident that the sorrow and pain will subside once they are confronted and healed.

It's kind of like an old water faucet that has not been used in some time. When it is first turned on, old water that has collected in the pipes comes pouring out. This water is warm, dirty and not very pleasant. But if the tap is left open, soon the water turns clearer, colder and before long it is available for us to drink to nourish our bodies.

So it is with the heart. When opened after being shut for some time, some unpleasant stuff needs to come out before we can tap the nourishment that is soon to follow. But if we are patient and we allow the heart to remain open, soon the heart begins to share its beauty with us, and nurture us with love.

3.

Love's first requirement is that it be given to ourselves.

We are not reactors and we are not victims, we are creators of our lives. If you are not consciously choosing your reaction to all situations, then you are being controlled by something other than your greatest desire for yourself. This will inevitably lead to a lack of love and happiness in your life.

No one can have your best interests in mind all of the time other than yourself. So you have to take responsibility for your happiness and the amount of love in your life. Love and happiness must become priorities in your life and the conscious object of your focus on a daily, even a momentary, basis.

If you do not love yourself completely, it is unlikely you will allow others to love you either, for you will always perceive that others love you the same way you love yourself. If you do not love yourself, then nobody will be able to love you enough. You will Inevitably place unrealistic expectations on others in your life to give you the love you so badly need.

To love completely you must first begin to love yourself. We cannot be ready to love another, with all of their doubts, fears and weakness, until we learn to love ourselves and embrace all of our own doubts, fears and weaknesses. Many of us have great difficulty in loving ourselves because subconsciously we do not feel we meet other's expectations. As children, often we received criticism from those closest to us and we found that our parents or friends were not happy unless we were complying with their demands or needs. This criticism subconsciously sent a message that we were not worthy of love unless we were meeting their expectations.

Growing up, we received the most love and acceptance

when we were conforming to the rules of the house. To meet these expectations, we learned to sacrifice our own needs and wants. When we become adults, however, nobody really teaches us that we must begin to reverse this process and begin taking responsibility for meeting our own needs and wants. Few teach us that it is emotionally healthy to meet our needs and wants, or that it is healthy to begin to distance ourselves from conformity to other people's ideas and beliefs about how we should be.

So many of us lose our way. We have given up too much of ourselves over time and we have not learned how to reclaim it. But reclaim it we must. It is the only way to increase our self-worth and self-esteem and begin to love ourselves completely. When we begin to make the best choices for ourselves, even if it may upset those around us, we take the first steps towards loving ourselves.

The world can be a deceptive place and our culture teaches us the exact opposite of true self-love. Popular culture spreads the message of living for the moment and seeking pleasure now at the cost of long-term happiness. In our magazines, our movies, and our television programs, infidelity, dishonesty, and selfishness are glamorized and elevated to such a level that people emulate these traits and believe that they are acting in their own self-interests by employing them.

However, what the movies and magazines never seem to portray is the cold, empty feeling that occurs when we act in this way and we deny our true essence – that of love and honesty. No one talks about the low self-esteem that inevitably results when we have been dishonest with our partners and engaged in a stolen evening with another. Or the loneliness we feel when the relationship we have betrayed, ends in distrust, anger or alienation. These are the results that linger with us and affect us long after the relationship with the other has ended.

While the momentary pleasure from some dishonest

events can be intense, once it leaves, as it is sure to do, it leaves a gaping hole in the soul. The dishonesty eats away at our souls like a cancer and we cannot stop the insecurity it creates no matter how capable we can become of ignoring the symptoms. Deep down, we begin to feel unworthy of the love of another, which further drives insecurity, self-destructive behaviors, and dishonesty until the downward, spiraling circle is complete. Pain and suffering, loneliness, insecurity and sorrow are the outcomes of this path — make no mistake about it.

The feelings generated by loving actions and honesty towards the self and others are deep and meaningful and flow from within. I begin to feel the sweetest sense of peace, happiness and contentment with myself. It is as if a wellspring of love emerges from within me that rises up and swallows my entire being. I become completely overwhelmed by a great sense of security, happiness, confidence and love. I know that it comes from knowing that I am being true to myself and who it is I want to be. There is no greater feeling in the world, for it completely fills every hole and gap in the soul that has been created by past, inconsistent choices. It is a healing power beyond description. It is pure love and it is the consequence of being true and honest to ourselves.

It is not easy to always act in a loving way to ourselves. The world does throw a lot of temptations and hurdles in the way. These hurdles and temptations are spiritually intentional and a necessary part of our experience. Often, it is only through the experience of the pain and sorrow that accompanies our inconsistent and dishonest choices that we learn the real value of honest choices. It is certainly by the comparison of the negative feelings generated by dishonest choices that we are able to measure, fully experience, and appreciate the grandeur and magnitude of our loving and honest choices.

You are presented every day with the opportunity to be consistent and honest with yourself and others, or to be dishonest. In our lives, the decision of who we are and who we want to be and whether we will act in accordance with this ideal is a moment-by-moment decision. This decision is often difficult. We become confused because of the contrasting messages we receive from friends, family, and our culture. But the beauty of life is that it presents us with the opportunity to experience and learn for ourselves. The time it takes to learn these lessons is irrelevant. We all have a different pace and a different path.

We cannot judge the path chosen by others or compare the path of another to our own. The only consideration we ought to make is whether the path we are on is the one we consciously choose to represent us, and whether it is taking us to where we want to go. If it is not, then we must begin to take responsibility for making changes in our decisions. We must begin to have the courage and fortitude to make hard choices, putting our long-term well-being and happiness over short-term pleasures. Only then will we begin to reap the benefits of loving ourselves in this essential way.

4.

Love and honesty are synonyms.

One of the most important acts of self-love we must do in order to learn to love ourselves, and ultimately love others, is to become one hundred percent honest. This does not mean mostly honest or honest most of the time. It means completely honest. Complete truth is absolutely necessary for complete love to enter the picture. Without total truth and honesty we act contrary to our essential nature, which is love and truth.

Those that are dishonest, devious, or deceitful to any degree can never experience complete love in their lives or be completely happy. Deep down they are deceiving others in order to receive love and acceptance. This deception is born out of fear, not love. In the presence of fear, love retreats.

There are many negative consequences that result from dishonesty. While many believe that the distrust of others is the worst consequence, in fact, the most negative consequence of dishonesty comes from the way in which we negatively affect ourselves. As George Bernard Shaw once remarked: "The liar's punishment is not in the least that he is not believed, but that he cannot believe anyone else." When we engage in a pattern of dishonesty in any relationship, not only do we destroy the foundation upon which that relationship is built, but we also contribute to our own demise. We color our view of all others with the same shades of dishonesty that we ourselves have. Cynicism, distrust, anger and resentment are inevitably a result of such behavior, and they are the earmarks of a dishonest relationship. Only when we are completely honest with ourselves and our partners do we build the foundation on which love can enter fully and completely.

More often than not, people lack the confidence to be honest. We often believe that we have to be something that we are not in order for others to love us. We do not feel good enough, smart enough, or confident enough, so we have to pretend to be those things to others. In so doing, we subconsciously believe that we will receive the love and acceptance we truly desire. The problem with this approach, however, is that it is dishonest. It is untruthful and it is not genuine.

As humans, we can intuitively sense when someone is being dishonest. Very few people are able to deceive all of the time. People who lie and present something different than who they really are cannot maintain the deceit forever. Eventually they slip and inconsistencies are noticed. When we try to obtain love from others by pretending to be something that we are not, we become what I refer to as a "Love Bandit." Love Bandits pretend and lie in order to receive love. They are insecure about themselves and they deceive to obtain at least some love and acceptance, even if it is not exactly the love they want. Love Bandits usually hurt themselves more than anyone else. They do not feel confident that people will love them for who they are, so they try to steal love by pretending to be who they are not.

Love bandits try to obtain love by unethical means; they are unfaithful in their relationships. They pretend to like something they do not or they pretend to dislike something they really like in order to be accepted or acceptable. Love Bandits suppress their real feelings, needs and wants, and they hide their true identity. Love Bandits do this hoping to be loved by people who they believe would not if they knew what they were truly like.

Love Bandit behavior leads to insecurity and a lack of love and acceptance. The lack of love comes when our partners, over time, begin to see the real us. Once they discover who we really are, they often leave - not because they reject who or what we really are, but because our lack of honesty now puts into question everything we have said, not only about ourselves, but also about them. How are they to know whether our feelings for them are real? How can they trust what we have told them in the past or what we might say in the future? How can they really know we love them, when we have lied to them about other things?

Love and acceptance cannot be gained dishonestly.

Lack of trust and honesty is the primary destroyer of our relationships, our self-image, and our quest for true love. When we fail ourselves by being deceitful and dishonest, we start to feel even more insecure about ourselves. This insecurity usually leads to more lying and more deceiving, and thus, a vicious cycle of personal destruction is created.

If, however, we are honest with who we are and what we are, a positive cycle is created. When we are honest and open with others about who we are, we are assured that others accept us for who we really are, otherwise they would not be in our life. We become genuine through our honesty, and as a result we develop confidence and authentic power: a divine sense of who we really are.

Becoming an honest person with our partners, friends and in our relationships will lead to one of two results. Either we will be rejected or accepted for who we really are. If we are accepted, then we know the accepting person is a true friend, or partner. These relationships will become stronger as a result of our honesty, for we will know that we are accepted and loved despite our faults. If, however, our friends or partners reject us, although we might feel a certain amount of pain, we will know that we have only lost someone who cannot accept us for who we really are.

As we become truthful about who we really are we may clear out some relationships that have been built on dishonesty. But in becoming truthful and honest, we make room for those that will be attracted to who we really are. The greatest thing about being yourself and being honest with who you are, is the confidence you gain knowing that the people who are now attracted to you are those that are attracted to the real you. This confidence fuels a continued desire to be honest, which in turn leads to more confidence. A positive cycle of self-love is created through this process. You begin to feel good about yourself for being yourself, and thus, you start loving yourself more. As you love yourself more, you feel more confident to be honest about who you are, which attracts more people into your life that truly love you for you. This breeds more love in your life, more confidence, and more honesty.

Our willingness to be completely honest to ourselves and others creates an upward spiral of love, confidence and security that magnifies immeasurably our self worth. It is here that love for self begins.

5.

There is no greater advice for you than that which lies within your own heart.

"There is something in every one of you that waits and listens for the sound of the genuine in yourself. It is the only true guide you will ever have. And if you cannot hear it, you will all of your life spend your days on the ends of strings that somebody else pulls." – Howard Thurman

One of the steps towards learning to love yourself is beginning again to listen to your heart. When we were children, listening to our heart was easy because our minds had not been loaded up with all of the negativity that so many others project onto us. As children, it was easy to laugh and easy to play. When we felt a negative emotion we expressed it immediately. Once the feeling was expressed, we returned quickly to play, joy and laughter.

As you begin the process of learning to love yourself you must begin to trust your feelings, intuitions and the promptings of your heart. The heart is that part of us where our best advice lies. The heart tells us the truth if we are prepared to listen to it. We must ask our hearts the most honest questions we can. Are we really happy? Do we make those choices that satisfy our hearts and souls in the long-term, or do we choose momentary pleasures that deep down we know are wrong for us? How do we feel about our relationships and our own needs and desires? Are they really being fulfilled? Have we communicated honestly with our partners? Are we living a life that is consistent with our beliefs? Are we being totally honest with ourselves?

The heart will answer these questions honestly because the heart can only operate in truth. The mind is quite clever and can justify many things our hearts would tell us are wrong. One only needs to look at the many horrors of history that have occurred and what man has been able to mentally or logically justify to see evidence of this. But the heart will not deceive and will not justify. It shows us honestly what is the correct path to follow.

The problem for many is that we have learned to stop listening to the truth of our hearts because the messages are often difficult to accept. It is easier to deceive ourselves and others than to be completely honest. It is easier to rationalize and justify than face the truth about ourselves. But the pain associated with truth never goes away until we are willing and able to face it. When we learn to place the heart at the center of our being as the prime decision-maker, love, peace and happiness return to our lives.

Listening to the heart means trusting your inner voice. All of us, at some time or another have had the sensation of "feeling" something about a situation that is not necessarily evident from the facts. This feeling is not to be confused with unwarranted anxiety that can be caused by insecurity or lack of self-esteem. Rather, it is a notion or a feeling about someone or a situation that we feel comes from deep within and sheds light on the situation we might not otherwise be able to see. This is the inner-voice and unfortunately many of us have learned to shut this inner voice down or turn it off completely. We often cast aside our intuition because it does not accord with society's view of how we **should** think or feel about a given situation.

Our world is largely comprised of the opinions of people, who without solutions to their own problems, try to justify their own bad decisions by convincing others to make similar choices. More often than not, these choices are not tied to principles, core values, or doing what is best for the soul, but rather are geared towards achieving the social acceptance of others.

Following inner wisdom leads to an alignment between the actions of a person and their truth about the subject of those actions. When people act consistently like this, they honor themselves and they validate their feelings and thoughts. This helps to create confidence, greater self-esteem and stronger self-love.

We must learn to love and trust ourselves before we can love and trust others. Trusting ourselves means listening to our inner voice, admitting to ourselves **our truth** of a situation and not denying or burying the truth because we find it too difficult to accept. In other words, trusting ourselves means letting go of the fear of being truthful, following our hearts, and having the courage to "let the chips fall where they may."

6.

How can I love me? Let me count the ways.

To love ourselves, we must learn to love our weaknesses, our so-called "bad stuff." There are many who have learned to negatively react to what they view as their bad traits or weaknesses. They deny that they exist, they repress associated feelings, they project these weaknesses onto others, they feel guilty, or they go overboard in opposite areas trying to compensate for these self-perceptions.

Learning to love ourselves means learning to love and accept all parts of our humanity. Emotions and behavior like anger, jealousy, envy, selfishness, and unhappiness are typical human emotions and reactions that we all experience. We cannot be loving, balanced and happy all of the time. It is okay to allow ourselves to experience these other emotions. If we insist on rejecting or repressing them, they build up inside until they surface with much more ferocity than they ever would have exhibited had we simply acknowledged them and dealt with them when they were originally felt.

We must recognize that negative emotions and traits are an essential part of our human experience. We must also learn that these "negative traits" can be channeled and utilized in ways that positively affect others. For example, that part of me which may be arrogant and egotistical is also the part of me that I can use to drive accomplishment of a deed or act in a way that benefits others. Or, that part of me that is needy of the acceptance and approval of others can also be that which motivates me to serve others.

We must learn to accept everything about ourselves, even what we view as the bad stuff. Then, we must learn to see the positive aspects of these traits and try to channel our energy into converting these negative traits or emotions into personal strengths. As we learn to accept the negative sides of our personalities we will become understanding and compassionate. We will understand why we feel them and, by our acknowledgment of them, we will clear the way for overcoming them. Not surprisingly, we will also clear the way for us to understand and feel compassion towards the weaknesses of others. This kind of connection with the self ultimately forms the food chain upon which true love feeds.

Learning to love ourselves also requires desire: desire to understand why we have difficulty loving ourselves, desire to understand the blocks we place on loving ourselves, and desire to overcome these obstacles. This desire is ultimately created when we decide to make love a priority in our lives. We usually decide to make love a priority in our lives when we are tired of feeling unloved or when we see the love others have and we want it for ourselves.

Like anything we want to accomplish, however, the pursuit of love requires effort as well as desire. We spend a lot of our time going to school, working at our jobs, entertaining ourselves and pursuing relationships. But how many of us consciously spend time each day pursuing love? How many of us take the time to develop rituals of love in our lives? Is it surprising that so few of us know what real love is? We must put time, effort and energy into bringing love into our lives.

One of the secrets to bringing self-love into our lives is becoming focused on the present. Each unfolding moment of your life presents an opportunity for love, but this opportunity is lost when we are living in the past or worried about the future. Love is a present-moment activity. Love reaches its full expression only when the conscious is situated in the here and now. Love cannot express itself fully in the past or the future, for these are domains of the mind. But in the present, the mind can let go and the heart can prevail. People underestimate the value of learning to absorb themselves in the present moment. When we engage in our passions – love, sex, music, sports, theater, reading – whatever it is that allows us to lose ourselves in the present moment, we are connecting with our inner self and creating an atmosphere of inner love. Learning to love yourself, therefore, requires that you become focused on the present.

One of the opportunities that love presents with present moment focus is appreciation and gratitude. These traits are excellent conduits for love, for they come from the heart and give to the heart. Life is one grand dichotomy and those that see the negative in it and those that see the positive in it are both right, for life presents both sides, the whole. The question you must decide for yourself, however, is which will you choose to acknowledge.

You can choose to focus upon the black lining or you can choose to see the silver lining. One brings an experience of pain, the other brings an experience of joy. One brings fear, the other love. One brings misery, the other happiness. All of these states of being are choices and each of us is free to choose what we will see and experience. Learning to appreciate and express gratitude are excellent ways to see the silver lining in life, to choose joy over pain, love over fear, and happiness over misery. When we appreciate and are grateful for all that is good in our lives, we cannot help but feel more love for ourselves.

To become truly loving of ourselves we must also abandon judgment. As we discussed earlier, all judgment is premature for it assumes knowledge of the final consequence of our actions or the actions of others. Yet, in all cases we have not seen the final act of the play. Therefore, we cannot make judgment. It is premature.

When you do things that do not represent who you really are, learn to quickly forgive yourself. Life is a process of creation and we cannot make the best choices in all situations. We cannot be perfect. Therefore, we must learn to forgive ourselves and move on. This moment and the next moment, despite any past mistakes we have made, are new opportunities to act in accordance with what we believe is the highest vision of ourselves. We have the opportunity to act differently today and that is a glorious opportunity. In each and every moment of every day we can decide anew who it is we want to be, and what actions we will take that represent the greatest and grandest aspects of our souls.

7.

The road to love of self is only ever blocked by us.

Learning to love ourselves is not an easy task. People who feel unloved, either consciously or subconsciously, resort to many different strategies to fill their vast need for love. Some pretend to be something they are not so they can receive love from those around them. Others try and accumulate power and attempt to control those around them as a defense mechanism to their own feelings of insecurity or vulnerability. Still others give away so much of themselves to please others and receive their acceptance that they completely lose themselves and grow increasingly cynical and resentful.

Whenever we engage in these types of behaviors to obtain acceptance from others, our interactions and relationships no longer have much to do with love, but rather are motivated by our insecurities and fears, and our intense desire to be accepted. Under such conditions, true love struggles to manifest itself.

True love of self exists in a different place. True love acknowledges fear, but lets go of it. True love recognizes the importance of honesty to self and others, despite the pain that might be caused by such truth, and accepts no compromise. True love is not afraid to acknowledge weakness, emotion or insecurity, knowing that by this very acknowledgment we in fact grow stronger.

True love recognizes that boundaries must be drawn and limits imposed. True love knows that being true, honest, and loving with self must come first before love can be freely given to others. True love does not try to dominate, control, deceive, misrepresent, hide, cover weaknesses or insecurities, or please too much. Rather, true love flows freely, it appreciates and is grateful for perceived good and bad. True love freely acknowledges the presence of insecurities, fears and weaknesses. Real love basks in the light of truth and gives itself as an unconditional gift to others.

All of us encounter roadblocks to love, loving and being loved. But the roadblocks are those that we have created. As Baba Ram Dass once commented, "If I see one dilemma with Western man, it's that he can't accept how beautiful he is. He can't accept that he is pure light, that he's pure love, that he's pure consciousness, that he's divine." Whether it is insecurity, dishonesty or fear, we often stumble when we come upon such roadblocks and we find it difficult for our love to flow. But love is our very essence and so it must flow. Eventually love will find a way to teach us its lessons so long as we are open to receive them.

To allow our love to flow more freely we must stop judging the weaknesses of others. Rather, we must begin to look with compassion upon others and try to understand them from their perspective, not ours. We must also stop blaming others for our circumstances. We must accept full responsibility for our state of being, and acknowledge that we have the power to change it. We must stop doubting the intentions and honesty of others and we must begin to act honestly ourselves. And finally, to allow our love to flow more freely, we must stop acting out of fear. These things block the flow of love in our lives.

Perhaps the most important rule to implement when you encounter a circumstance, situation or person that challenges your ability to be loving is one offered by Benjamin Shield: "We continue the journey – not by overpowering something *outside* ourselves, but by letting go of something *inside* ourselves." This letting go of "something inside" is accomplished by being honest with ourselves and others, keeping our hearts open, risking being hurt by exposing our true feelings, desires and needs, releasing past pains, and allowing others to love us.

We have all had experiences of hurt that create in us the

fear of loving and letting go. These experiences make it difficult for us to love. But we must face these fears consciously, we must recognize and admit that they are only the consequences of past pain, and we must acknowledge that they block the flow of love. By opening ourselves up to this process we can begin to break down the barriers of past pain, fear and insecurity and start to loosen the tight grasp of ego on our identities.

Once we get out of the way of ourselves, we allow our natural essence – our love – to flow freely. As long as we continue to allow fear to enter our lives, however, we will continue to block the flow of love.

The next time you are faced with a difficult choice or decision, rather than act out of fear, imagine what choice you would make if you had everything and you were being everything you ever wanted to be in life. The choice you would make if you were being everything you wanted to be in life will ultimately be the right choice, for you will be acting in accordance with your grandest desires for yourself.

When we consciously act as we want to be, we clear the way for love to flow. We begin to love who we are and admire the strength and courage we are showing ourselves by doing what we know is right. And ultimately, we fill our lives so full with love that we begin to feel the safety and security necessary to share our love freely with others.

When we love ourselves in this way something else begins to happen. Life begins to be magical again. Our heart starts to encourage us more, for it knows we are listening. We become more willing to take risks for we trust that we will respond to all situations with love. Our souls begin to encourage us to take new paths that we never thought before were possible. And we begin to find our lives filled with sudden moments of inspiration and spontaneous feelings of love and security.

Each day becomes a glorious chance for us to fully embrace and experience the totality of being that love offers.

8.

I love because I choose to and want to, not because I need to. I love for the joy that loving brings me and others, not for the return of love. If others love me in return, then I am blessed and I appreciate such love. If others do not return my love, it does not matter, for by the very act of loving I have defined who it is I am and want to be.

When we are able to look upon the weaknesses of another with love, understanding and compassion, we develop the ability to look upon ourselves the same way. In other words, we experience the love we share with others. The more easily we do so with others, the more easily we can do so for ourselves. Invariably, when we cannot love others easily, we have a problem loving ourselves.

There is a maxim that states that what we do not like in others is usually something we do not like in ourselves. For a long time I did not believe this. I felt I could easily detect in others traits or qualities that bothered me, but were not traits that I possessed. I was, as they say, in denial. I first begin to notice this fact when I began to look at negative qualities of others that **did not** bother me. Why was there a difference? Why could I look at some negative qualities of others with compassion, understanding and patience, and yet with other qualities I would become reactive, emotional, and disdainful? I learned that what upsets us about the behavior of others is either something that we do not like about ourselves, or it causes a reaction or responsive feeling within us that is something we do not like.

Let me give you some examples. If you are the kind of person that is always sweet and patient and never loses your temper and I accuse you of flying off the handle and being completely unreasonable, you are likely to smile at me politely and think of me as ignorant. However, if I accuse you of being emotionless, unresponsive and lacking passion, you may react to me quite negatively. The difference is that the second criticism probably hits closer to home, while the first does not.

If you are a jealous person who was dating someone who could not be entirely trusted, their behavior could likely cause your jealousy to come to the forefront of your emotions. You may react to them harshly, criticizing their behavior, when in fact your reaction is more of a commentary on your jealousy and insecurity. If you did not have a problem with jealousy, or if you were secure with yourself, then you would react to their issue of trust in a loving, compassionate, and understanding way.

As I began to understand and heal aspects of myself (of course, I am still in the process), and I learned to love and accept myself despite having habits or behaviors that I knew I wanted to change, I started to feel differently towards others with habits or behaviors that previously caused me problems. Where I once became ill-tempered or impatient when others acted towards me with these behaviors or habits, I began to feel more compassion, understanding and patience.

We all have areas of weakness, things we can change and things we would like to change, but feel like we cannot. We do not need to be perfect, for no one is. We must learn to accept our imperfections and weaknesses by recognizing how they can be utilized in a positive way. As we do, we become tolerant of them in ourselves, we empower ourselves with love to change them, and we start to feel more accepting and loving of ourselves. Learning to love yourself and accept yourself as you are, weaknesses and all, opens the door to allow you to start loving others and their less than perfect parts.

In one of the songs of the Broadway play *Les Misérables*, there is a line that says "to love another person is to see the face of God." Love is our very nature and is the true essence of all life. Love is God, and God is love. The expression of real love towards another human being is the most elevated and divine action a human being can take. In simple terms, when we show our love towards others we are acting divinely, we are acting like God. And when we act like God, we will feel like God.

One of the simplest maxims that is common to the themes of all great teachers on love is that love returns to us to the same degree and extent that we give it. Quite simply, if you want more love in your life, give more love. How do you do this? Become aware of the needs of those to whom you are trying to express love. Awareness is created by attention and when you are talking to a loved one, try to truly listen to what it is they want, not what you think they need. Too often we make judgments about what we think our partners need, instead of asking them and listening to their answers. It does not matter if we think they are wrong about their need or not. It is enough that they perceive the need. If we truly love them, then we will address that perception and try to satisfy it without compromising what is important to us.

In every circumstance, situation and personal encounter of your life you have the opportunity to love. Perhaps it is not obvious, such as when someone says something offensive or demeaning to you, or when someone acts in an unloving way towards you. But the fact of the matter is you can always choose to respond in love and, by doing so, significantly increase the love that is in your life.

"But" you might say, "what do I do when someone hurts me, when someone makes me feel so angry or upset?" These feelings can be felt honestly, but to act upon them impulsively is to ignore their source. Nobody **makes** us feel any way. Nobody **makes** us angry or upset. True, they may act in a way that triggers these typical reactions, but the choice of the reaction is still ours to make. Despite how you act towards me, I can choose to react with love, patience, and understanding. This was the example Jesus gave us with his life. Even in his final moments, when he was being tortured and murdered, he did not react with love because he was born that way, he reacted with love because he made a conscious choice to do so. You, too, can consciously choose loving reactions to adversity in your life and rise above the frailties and insecurities of others.

Recognize the lack of self-acceptance and love that underlies the negative actions of others. Respond with kindness and love to situations where negative actions are presented and you will begin to feel a much greater sense of the divine power that exists within you. The single most powerful question you can ask yourself in any situation you encounter is how would you wish to be treated if the situation were reversed. This does not mean how you would expect to be treated, or how you deserve to be treated, but rather how you would wish to be treated. The answer to this question is almost always the most loving alternative that exists as a solution to any situation.

This answer is embodied in a principle has been in existence since the beginning of time, and it forms an integral part of every major religion. Whether it is called The Golden Rule, the Law of Karma, or anything else, if we always acted in a manner that we would want to be treated, our response to the most difficult situations would be a loving one.

Difficult circumstances, events or people are the very opportunities by which we choose to either fill our lives with love, or demonstrate that we are not ready for love. It is easy to love those that are nice to us or who act in accordance with our wishes.

But the true test of how important love is to us comes when we are faced with whether or not to choose love in response to unkindness, thoughtlessness, or unloving behavior. When faced with such choices in our lives we need to learn to identify them immediately and recognize that our loving response is that which will elevate our souls and fill our lives with love.

Remember that loving others is as much a choice as loving ourselves. Despite how another person may act towards us we can always choose to love in return. This does not mean we tolerate abuse or mistreatment in any way. In fact it means the opposite. Loving someone means not allowing them to engage in behavior that will ultimately damage their self-esteem and your own. Loving someone also means that when they act toward us in a manner that we do not understand or that we may feel is unkind, we react with compassion, understanding, and a deeper motivation to understand the intent and true motivation behind the action.

I know that when other people act in ways that seem hurtful or uncaring, that they are susceptible to the same feelings of anger, insecurity, fear and confusion that I feel. I also know that if I understood them completely and could see their upbringing, failures and their fears, I would probably respond with more love and compassion, because I would better understand them. I would probably not judge them, but rather would empathize with them. True love for another demands such understanding and compassion. True love for another requires us to want the best for them and their potential, despite the fact that this outcome may differ from what we had hoped for or expected. It is surprising to me the number of times I have wanted a specific outcome with someone that I knew deep down was different than an outcome they wanted. As I have become more aware of the issue of love and its importance in my life, I am learning to let go of this form of expectation and I am learning to let love move in its own way.

Truly loving others means allowing, and in fact encouraging, them to pursue their desires and fulfill their potential, even if it results in an outcome that differs from our own desires. In the end, love requires that we allow others to be who they want to be, not what we would have them be.

9.

Love first!

Whether it is called the Golden Rule, the Law of Karma, or simply just good horse sense, the principle of treating others the way we would want to be treated is an enduring principle that forms a central theme of almost all value-based philosophies. When we think about how we would want to be treated before we act, and then we act in accordance with what we would desire, we will rarely act in an unloving manner.

We all crave kind, compassionate acts of love in our lives. All people want to be treated with respect, kindness, understanding and love. And usually we are happy to give these things to those that treat us in a similar manner. However, unconsciously, we often insist that the other party act in this manner before we are prepared to respond in kind. This is called conditional behavior and it exacts a cost from us as well as from the other party. The cost we pay is being closed, guarded, suspicious, and, in reality, unloving.

I have a philosophy I recommend to overcome this type of conditional loving: **love first.** Look at each person, situation and event in your life as an opportunity to **love first.** Love not for the potential return of love, but rather for the feelings of confidence, security, and "higher self" that will be a natural consequence to your unconditional loving action.

Before you require anything of anyone, **love first.** When someone treats you harshly or negatively, **love first.** When someone demonstrates an action that appears unloving, **love first** in response. **Love first** and you will attract loving people and actions into your life. **Love first** and love will always be a priority in your life.
Love first and the first thing in your life will be love.

Loving first means we must approach all situations and all individuals with kindness, despite the difficult task this sometime is. Others may advise you to respond in kind when someone is being difficult, or will tell you not to be naïve and allow someone to take advantage of you. But remember that all responses come at a price, and although you may be tempted to respond in kind to someone who is acting in an unloving manner towards you, there is a long-term cost.

By responding in an unloving manner in any situation, we impose blocks to love flowing freely in our lives. With such blocks in place, loving others and being loved becomes more difficult. Imposing such blocks also leads to more insecurity, fear and distrust. Responding to unloving situations or people with love, however, creates just the opposite kind of cycle. We become empowered. When someone acts in an unloving way toward you, rather than focusing on the unloving action, focus instead on the opportunity that the unloving action creates! You now have the opportunity to show how loving a person you really are! You can now respond with love, understanding and kindness.

Choosing to react to unloving situations or people in anger or unkindness will make you feel weak, insecure and upset. Choosing to respond with love and kindness will significantly increase your sense of personal strength and power. This is why people like Jesus and Ghandi became so powerful. They learned to respond to unkindness and hate with love and understanding. This made their sense of personal strength and power increase to a point where people began to take notice. The more they were hated, the more they responded in love and the greater became their strength and power. This is why the most powerful people this world has ever known are those that possessed the greatest capacity to love.

Begin to be aware of your reactions to difficult circumstances or people. Look at every event as an opportunity to grow and develop yourself. Begin responding whenever you can to all situations with forgiveness, understanding and compassion. Rise above the unloving and unkind actions of others and begin responding with love. **Love first**, and as you do, your sense of personal strength will grow and you will become more empowered than you have ever imagined possible.

10.

Love is not a limited resource, but rather is a wellspring of unlimited supply.

Eric Fromm once stated: "Infantile love follows the principle: I love because I am loved. Mature love follows the principle: I am loved because I love." We sometimes find it hard to unilaterally love others, but once we do it we always feel rewarded. That is one of the secrets of love. The lover is the one who benefits most from the love she gives. The single, greatest action you can take to increase the love in your life is to give love away. We have love in our lives in direct proportion to the love that we ourselves give.

In retrospect, loving others seems easy. And it is. Loving is a habit that like all habits gets easier with practice. Be more affectionate, be kind, thank others for their kindness, do an act of service, give of yourself – not only to those that you believe deserve your love, but also to those you believe do not. The more love you give, the more you will receive and the less needy of love you yourself will become.

One of the simplest ways in which we can demonstrate our love for others is the simple act of gratitude. Recognizing and thanking others for their acts of kindness, thoughtfulness or love is a simple way to return the positive feelings that the act of love or kindness generated. Gratitude also brings to the giver greater happiness. We cannot feel unhappy or "out of love" when we are expressing gratitude towards another, because gratitude to unhappiness is like light is to darkness. In the presence of one, the other cannot exist.

Too often we assume that people are aware of our gratitude or appreciation without the need for us to express it. This assumption, however, is both misplaced and irrelevant. Even if others know we are grateful, no harm is caused by the reiteration of our gratitude. It merely emphasizes the point. Furthermore, any assumption that our gratitude is understood is susceptible to error. It is possible that someone else could be feeling too insecure or unloved to assume that we appreciate their act of love. If you believe that love is the highest priority in life, why take the chance? Make the statement of gratitude towards someone who treats you kindly. Let someone else know how much you appreciate their love and their actions. Acknowledge the good deeds of others that make your life better. William Arthur Ward once said: "Feeling gratitude and not expressing it is like wrapping a present and not giving it." Gratitude is a gift we should share freely with all. The spread of gratitude is infectious and an instrumental part of creating an atmosphere where love flows freely.

Another way we can love others is by listening without judgment. As Helmut Thielicke once declared: "Tell me how much you know of the sufferings of your fellow men and I will tell you how much you have loved them." We love others when we listen to what it is that they most want to share with us. Often, when people close to us share their thoughts, feelings or emotions, we are quick to respond with our advice. Or, if we have chosen to react to the information by feeling insecure, then we will typically respond by seeking reassurance. However, one of the most loving things we can do is to simply listen to and support them without giving judgment or advice. Listening empathetically and supportively creates a safe environment where others feel secure enough to share their feelings, ambitions and fears.

Responding to others with "advice" or our "counsel" when it is not asked for, however, creates an environment where people may feel threatened, insecure or even more fearful. We can give love to others by learning to just listen to them without commentary or criticism. Listen to them without probing questions, without opinion and without judgment, unless they seek these things from you. When you know that someone is opening their heart and soul to you, whoever they are, make a conscious effort to respond only with support, understanding and encouragement.

Another way we love others is to serve them and make sacrifices for them. Do you know what sacrifice is? Have you sacrificed anything in your own life for the love of another? What is true sacrifice? We often hear stories in the news of very wealthy individuals who donate large amounts of money to charities. In fact, not long ago we heard in the news of the donation of over one billion dollars to charity by a very wealthy billionaire. Do you think this is sacrifice? Perhaps it is.

When I think of sacrifice I am reminded of the story of the Pandava brothers, first told a very long time ago:

> After the battle of Kurukshetra the five Pandava brothers performed a great sacrifice and made very large gifts to the poor. All people expressed amazement at the greatness and richness of the

sacrifice, and said that such a sacrifice the world had never seen before. But, after the ceremony, there came a little mongoose, half of whose body was golden, and the other half brown; and he began to roll on the floor of the sacrificial hall.

He said to those around, "You are all liars; this is no sacrifice."

What!" they exclaimed, "you say this is no sacrifice; do you not know how much money and jewels were poured out to the poor and every one became rich and happy? This was one of the most wonderful sacrifices any man ever performed."

But the mongoose said: "Once there was a village, and in it there dwelt a poor Brahmin with his wife, his son, and his son's wife. They were very poor and lived on small gifts made to them for preaching and teaching. There came in that land a three years' famine, and the poor Brahmin suffered more than ever. When the family had starved for days, the father brought home one morning a little barley flour, which he had been fortunate enough to obtain, and he divided it into four parts, one for each member of the family. They prepared it for their meal, and just as they were about to eat, there was a knock at the door. The father opened it, and there stood a guest.

The poor Brahmin said, 'Come in, sir; you are welcome.' He set before the guest his own portion of the food, which the guest quickly ate and said, 'oh sir, you have killed me; I have been starving for ten days, and this little bit of food has but increased my hunger.'

Then the wife said to her husband, 'Give him my share,' but the husband said 'Not so.' The wife however insisted, saying 'Here is a poor man, and it is our duty as householders to see that he is fed, and it is my duty as a wife to give him my portion, seeing that you have no more to offer him.' Then, she gave her share to the guest, which he ate, and then said he was still burning with hunger.

So the son said, 'Take my portion also; it is the duty of a son to help his father fulfill his obligations.' The guest ate that, but remained still unsatisfied; so the son's wife gave him her portion also. That was sufficient and the guest departed, blessing them. That night those four people died of starvation. A few granules of flour had fallen on the floor; and when I rolled my body on them, half of it became golden as you see. Since then I have been travelling all over the world hoping to find another sacrifice like that, but nowhere have I found one. That is why I say this is no sacrifice."

We all instinctively know that it is not the amount of the gift that determines the level of sacrifice, but rather the effect the gift has on the giver that matters. If we look closely at the needs of others, we will find countless opportunities to sacrifice and serve. Few of them will require the giving of our lives. Acting in service or sacrifice will always increase the love in our lives and the lives of those to whom the service or sacrifice is made. One of the best examples I know of how to serve and love others is the way we generally love our children. For them, we would do anything and sacrifice everything. Do we ask anything in return? Usually not. We gladly work for them, love them and care for them without thought of return.

In aspiring towards unconditional love, we must learn to love everyone the way we love our children: without thought of return. Learn to love loving others. Take delight in doing something for others and not getting anything back. Look for opportunities to help others without their knowing it. You will find that the feelings generated by random, unconditional acts of love and kindness are addictive and will motivate you to further acts of love. I know I am becoming more loving when I can feel love for complete strangers. As absurd as this may sound, when traveling on buses, or planes, I can pick out any stranger sitting close by that I have no reason to be attracted to, and within myself try to feel love for that person. I imagine them with many of the vulnerabilities and sensitivities that I feel and I try to feel compassionate towards them as a fellow human being. At times, I will imagine embracing them in a caring, loving way, or I will see myself helping them in some way. Whenever I can do this successfully I feel loving inside and loving those around me becomes much easier.

Another significant part of learning to love others is allowing others to love us. Many people have great difficulty in accepting kind deeds or actions from others, or "taking a compliment" as they say. These people usually only feel comfortable when they are giving, not receiving. Pope John XXIII tells us, however: "Never hesitate to hold out your hand; never hesitate to accept the outstretched hand of another." We must recognize that when we sidestep an offer of help from a friend, or we joke in response to a compliment paid, or we reject the loving behavior of another person, we rob them of the joy that comes from giving and loving.

In the same way we feel a sense of happiness and love when we act in a loving manner, so, too, do those around us who wish to act in a loving manner. Therefore, we show great love to others when we allow them to love us. Remember that the essence of life is love, and love in its natural state ebbs and flows through all things. Love is hindered and ultimately reduced when we block its flow – either out or in. To become truly loving beings, therefore, we must allow others to also express their love toward us.

In the end, the true test of our potential to love others is determined by the way we treat those that we believe are not necessarily deserving of our love or those that treat us in unloving ways. Like a true friend who proves his or her friendship during troubled times, when we learn to love in all situations and towards all people, we become truly loving human beings.

Love is not a limited resource, but, rather, is a wellspring of unlimited supply. Love multiplies by itself and upon itself. When you can love and feel yourself loving something about anyone and everyone, then love will take over and become you.

11.

Loving relationships are the mirrors by which we see our shadows.

The greatest mirror to our true self is that which is provided by a relationship. When we allow ourselves to become close to someone and we are willing to expose our inner selves, we allow ourselves to look in a mirror of sorts. Within the confines of a relationship we are forced to face all of our doubts, fears, and insecurities. No one can point out our faults and weaknesses better than a life partner. With them, we are forced to face our intentions and our ability to love on a daily basis. Relationships become, therefore, the vehicles by which we see that part of ourselves that we often try to hide, our shadows if you will.

For example, partners who know us best are not afraid to confront us with inconsistencies in our behavior that result from our lack of honesty. Our partners interact with other potential partners at work and at play almost every day, forcing us to face potential abandonment or rejection. Partners who deeply love and care for us force us to face the fear that we could one day lose this love and care. Partners who strive to better themselves make us question the expectations we have for ourselves. Partners who put a lot of effort towards making our relationship with them work cause us to examine our own intentions with respect to the relationship. Partners who give us love unconditionally allow us to consider the depth of our own love and our ability to share it. Partners who do not give us much love force us to examine how much love we have for ourselves, and our ability to love unconditionally in return.

Relationships truly are a mirror to our souls and, more than any other vehicle, provide the best opportunity for us to grow our ability to love. People often struggle to accept the insights that being in a relationship provides. Rather than reflect on that part of themselves that is exposed by a partner's behaviors or words, some people often only feel that others are "letting them down" or "hurting them." Sometimes people do legitimately let us down or hurt us with their words or actions, but what we perceive as being let down or hurt is someone shining the mirror so strongly that we see something scary, like a deep, hidden fear, that we find difficult to accept.

Let me give you an example. If I suggest to a partner in a spirited discussion that she is a murderer, she is likely to ignore my comments or laugh. Why? Because she knows deep within her that nothing could be farther from the truth, so my comment is not threatening. However, If I comment to her that her provocative behavior towards other men (assuming she does act this way) suggests a deficiency in her self-esteem, she is likely to react quite negatively and express anger, rejection, or disappointment.

Both comments could be considered offensive. If she is totally secure with herself and never acts provocatively towards other men, then she is likely to laugh as easily to my comment about her self-esteem as she did to my comment about her murderous tendencies. However, if she believes that she may have low self-esteem and she knows deep down inside that she does in fact act provocatively towards other men to get their attention, then my comment will strike a chord and she is more likely to react negatively.

By pointing out our weaknesses partners do not "let us down." They are simply holding up to us a mirror from which we cannot escape a view of our weaknesses. Once we begin to recognize and acknowledge this fact, however, we can begin the process of change. Change occurs when we are willing to acknowledge our weaknesses and take responsibility for them. Change occurs when we do not try to avoid issues by focusing on our partner's behaviors. Change occurs when we become secure enough to look to our partner for help in resolving or dealing with our weaknesses. Acting in this way, our relationships become an awesome vehicle for personal growth and development.

For many that consciously or subconsciously repress issues about weaknesses, coming face to face with them can be frightening. To progress and grow in our love, however, we must be willing to look in the mirror. We must face ourselves honestly, ask questions to and about ourselves, and we must listen and accept the truth of the answers we find.

The relationship is one place where we have the opportunity to do this work. If we are lucky, we have a partner who is also aware of this process and who wants to work with us patiently and lovingly and within the context of the partnership. In this way, love and the relationship become very powerful forces for healthy and healing change in our lives.

12.

Loving relationships will inevitably fail if they are not built upon complete honesty.

The only way you can truly love someone else is to present honestly who you are. Often in an attempt to initiate or preserve relationships, we try to be something that we are not. We try to be something that we believe the other person desires. When we do this in relationships we are not acting in love either for ourselves or for the other person, but rather we are building a relationship based upon deceit. Love cannot co-exist with deceit.

To love another demands that we present who we really are to them. This gives them the opportunity to make a choice about whether they are comfortable being with who we really are. When we are less than honest about ourselves and what we present to others, we strip from them the opportunity to make decisions based on facts. We trick them into decisions based on untruth. How can we believe love will thrive in such a relationship?

We must begin to connect with who and what we really are, and strip away the masks that we build to protect ourselves from rejection. The fear of rejection is why we build these masks, but more often than not rejection results from the inconsistencies that others see in us when we pretend to be something that we are not. In order to find true love, we must drop the masks, shed the false roles and pretenses we create, and be willing to expose our true feelings and our true selves. Only then will we know that others accept and love us for who we really are. This is the way to build loving and lasting bonds with another human being. Honesty will pave the way for loving relationships to flourish in our lives.

Honesty means that we are open and frank in our communication with others. If you feel you cannot be honest about your feelings, then in essence you are minimizing the importance of those feelings and you are demonstrating the fact that you are in a relationship that is not safe or secure enough to discuss how you really feel. In such relationships, you will have a hard time developing intimacy. Ultimately, you are likely to feel anger or resentment towards yourself or your partner, and such resentment or anger will threaten the continuation of the relationship.

It is not always easy to discuss topics or issues that we know will bother our friends or loved ones. Some people in fact believe that not discussing feelings that might hurt or disappoint a partner is a loving act, and act of sacrifice. The complete opposite is true. Not speaking honestly is deceptive and is an unloving act, for it deprives both parties of the opportunity to overcome the problem. It deprives relationships from the opportunity to overcome perceptions and the real hurdles that exist that deny love from evolving further.

Honest communication is an absolute, essential ingredient to a loving relationship. If you do not, or cannot, speak honestly about your actions, feelings, dreams, desires or thoughts within your relationship, then deep love and trust cannot be present. If these things are not present, then it is likely that the relationship is based on something else other than real love, like security or need. Such relationships are likely to fail once one of the parties to the relationship heals or resolves their need. It is then that they will begin to desire a real loving relationship that is based on honest communication.

Relationships based on love and trust are nurtured and built by overcoming hurdles in a mature and open way with someone that shares your desire to grow together. This is how love between two people is created. If one party to a relationship decides to hide his or her feelings to prevent such obstacles, true love cannot grow for the opportunities for development are hidden or removed. Although it is difficult, speaking honestly with one another lets the other party know that you trust them as a person and you trust them to deal with your weaknesses.

If you cannot be completely honest with someone in a relationship, then you have not yet learned how to love. The relationships you build will be unstable for they will be based on false pretenses. This instability will cause insecurity and will inevitably drive further dishonesty. The only cure for this negative cycle, and the only way to build truly loving relationships, is to become honest. You must begin to value personal honesty and integrity more than you value any relationship. Only then will your relationships allow true love to express itself. Remember always that your ability to speak honestly with others is a direct reflection of the degree of care and love you have for, or can give to, that person and to yourself.

13.

To create a loving relationship, you must love yourself first.

Although it may conflict with the views about relationships you have had in the past, one of the most important elements to a successful relationship is learning to love yourself first. By this I do not mean selfish, pleasure-seeking, ego-satisfying love. But rather, I mean unconditionally loving and accepting who you are. You must be willing to accept yourself to a point where you feel comfortable exhibiting your "self" in a true light to others. If you cannot yet do this, your relationships will struggle. This self-acceptance does not come from the acceptance of you by others. Rather, it comes from making your thoughts, words and actions consistent with who you really are. It comes from representing to others exactly who you are.

Once you have eliminated the misrepresentation of your "self" to others, and you show only that part of yourself that is real and honest, you will gain an enormous amount of confidence because you will feel freedom from the burden of hypocrisy. You will become at peace with yourself and you will know that the love and acceptance you receive from others is based on a true representation of your self, and not from a false presentation.

With this new sense of confidence and security, you will begin to stop taking the actions that insecure people, people who have not learned to love themselves, take. You will stop being paranoid that people who profess their love to you are really after something else. You will stop subconsciously forcing others to prove their love to you. You will stop taking desperate actions to hang on to the love and acceptance you receive from others. And you will stop worrying about whether you meet the expectations of others. Being free from the chains of insecurity, and the need to have others constantly reinforce your feelings of security, you will have the time and the ability to give to your relationships unconditionally. The once negative spiral of insecurity will give way to a positive cycle of nourishment, security and love.

Although relationships can and should hold a place of great importance in our lives, they should never take priority over our true natures. The moment we love another more than we love ourselves, we risk damaging the relationship and ourselves. We cannot love another until we love ourselves first, and we prioritize our values over anything or anyone else. If we compromise that which is important to us for the love of another, we are saying in essence that we are not worthy of greater love, of unconditional love. We also demonstrate to others that our values are not that important, that we are not that important, else why would we be willing to compromise them? How can we expect others to love and honor us more than we love ourselves? We cannot.

By elevating our values over relationships, however, we demonstrate honor and love for ourselves. When we honor and love ourselves, it is easier to love others, for we are no longer dependent on the love and acceptance of others to feel good about who we are. We will love ourselves all that is needed. Ultimately, it is easier to give away something that we believe we hold in abundance. Furthermore, as we love and honor ourselves, our partners will necessarily feel the same level of respect and honor that we have for ourselves. If they do not, they are not likely to remain as our partners for long. Love, honor and respect are infectious, and human experience teaches that we receive what we expect of ourselves.

You have an obligation in life and relationships to be yourself. To do otherwise seriously risks your emotional stability and spiritual growth and will inevitably doom the relationships you enter. This becomes more difficult to do if you have not been true to yourself in the past. But despite the difficulty, you must simply be who you are. If you are not yourself in your relationships, the relationship will crumble once you begin to fail at being who the other party wants or expects you to be. And fail you will, as no one can maintain the pretense of being something they are not forever.

Becoming your true self in a relationship means learning to "let go" and not trying to "force" relationships. Anyone who has ever tried to keep another person loving them will tell you it is a futile task in the long run. The desire "to keep" someone loving you is usually coupled with a willingness to compromise parts of yourself and your honesty in order to continue the supply of love. It is an endless battle that drains a person's essence and leaves them feeling emotionally spent and unable to give. This behavior is also usually perceived by the other party in the relationship, and leads to them feeling insecure about who and what you are, thus further destabilizing the relationship.

Release the need and desire to have people love you. Learn to love yourself and this release will become much easier. Focus instead on what you can control – the ability to express and show love to yourself and others.

Doing so will set your soul free.

14.

Relationships are the vehicles by which we manage the defining of our souls.

No one ever forces you to be un-loving. You only choose, consciously or unconsciously, to be un-loving in a given situation. You completely control your ability to love. The sooner this lesson is learned in life, the sooner you can begin to focus on loving. As you focus on loving others, a funny thing happens: you end up receiving more love than you could ever possibly give.

Learn to make the giving of love, rather than the receiving of love, the object of your focus. So many of us approach relationships from a vantage point of what we receive from them, rather than what we give to them. It is no surprise there is so much unhappiness in relationships. When we believe we have stopped receiving from the relationship, or in more common terms "when we have grown apart," we are often quick to move on.

The cycle of relationships, however, in many ways is like the cycle of life itself. In the beginning of our lives we are in a constant state of dependence on others. Be it parents, teachers, friends, or leaders, we are like walking sponges that soak up the thoughts, words and actions of others for our benefit. But at some point in our lives, the pendulum swings and the responsibility for us to give back and positively affect others the way we have been positively affected begins. As we mature, hopefully the desire to give replaces the need to receive.

The same is true in relationships. Adapting the famous words of U.S. president John F. Kennedy, ask not what your relationship can do for you, rather ask what you can do for your relationship. In more modern terms, the author Wayne Dyer has stated, "love is the ability and willingness to allow those that you care for to be what they choose for themselves without any insistence that they satisfy you."

When we reach the point of a relationship where we begin to feel that we do not receive what we should be receiving, rather than walk away, we should first ask ourselves what we have been giving to the relationship. Are there opportunities to give love? If there are, perhaps it not yet time to leave. If, however, we cannot give love back, or we are somehow prevented from loving our partners, or we know in our hearts that the most loving action we can do is to give them space and love them from a distance, then we can and should feel more at peace to leave.

Established relationships are the ideal place to begin the practice and art of unconditional loving. If we cannot love someone who has once loved and cared for us, how can we ever hope to love someone with whom we do not share such bonds? Perhaps the person to whom we demonstrate such love may not warmly receive it - or may in fact reject it. But before we ever walk away, we should learn to love. Otherwise walking away will become a dominant theme in our lives. There are not many individuals who will respond negatively to our love if it is truly given without condition over time.

Relationships are the vehicles by which we manage the defining of our souls. It is through our relationships with everything – people, objects, nature, events, etc., that we are created and defined, and we learn to express our true selves. Consequently, you should appreciate and bless all relationships, especially those that challenge you. So often these are the relationships that we want to run away from, to find other more comfortable replacements, yet these are the very relationships that ultimately help us the most to define ourselves and demonstrate our highest potential. Remember that **who you are with** is much less important than **how you are with them**. Unless you learn to perfect the "how," changing the "who" may not matter much.

Many of us strive towards having relationships without problems or issues. First of all, I am unaware of any relationship that at one time or another does not experience difficulty. In an effort to avoid conflict, some people in relationships have learned not to communicate or connect with the other party. Often they bury the real expression of themselves inside. When this happens, there is no relationship. It dies. And passion dies with it. Problems and issues can help a relationship to thrive, if both parties are committed to their resolve and are willing to adopt a mature form of communication to address them.

Relationships that have the best chance for survival are those in which **both** parties worry more about their **own** contributions than that of their partners; in which **both** parties focus more on ways to love the other and make the other feel more secure, than on how they are being loved or how they can feel more secure. Thriving relationships are those in which **both** parties look to solve problems in their relationship by opening their hearts and contributing love, understanding and kindness, rather than closing down or simply seeking the receipt of these things.

If you want to evaluate the likelihood that the relationship you are in will survive and grow, evaluate the level of love, understanding and kindness you bring to the relationship and analyze your desire to contribute these things. The chance of survival of your relationships directly correlates with the desire you have to contribute love, understanding and kindness to them, and the level to which you actually do.

Remember, however, to love for love's sake and not for security. If you love another in the hopes that your love will guarantee the security of the relationship, then you are destined for disappointment. Security of relationship is an illusion. It is a demand of the ego, not of the soul. There is no guarantee of involvement. Despite everything you may do to ensure the continuation of any relationship, random acts or the actions of others can cause any relationship to end. Despite how much we sacrifice or compromise to keep a relationship going, our partners could walk out the door tomorrow, be hit by a car, and be killed. Or, they may decide for reasons of their own, despite what we have given to the relationship, that they wish for it to cease, for it no longer serves their needs or their growth. If our sense of well-being or love is dependent on a relationship, then our lives will be shattered if and when the relationship ends.

    The only relationship you can control is the one you have with yourself. Despite what happens around you, you will always be there. That is why your values, your needs and loving yourself must take precedent in your life, and why you should not compromise yourself. Once you have learned to love and value the relationship you have with yourself, all other relationships can be treated as gifts.

    Enjoy them for what they are. Value and appreciate them each and every day that you have them. Nurture and sustain them with loving action, not for the return of love, but rather for the joy that you will receive when you give your love unconditionally. Relationships are the tools by which our characters are built. They are the vehicles through which we can express the best part of ourselves.

15.

True love makes no home for the ego.

The human heart, at its highest potential, has the ability to look upon anyone with tenderness, mercy and understanding. It does not judge the negative actions of others, but rather, tries to understand the pain that motivates such actions. It does not respond in kind to expressions of anger, hurt or rage, but rather recognizes the underlying fear that inspires these emotions and responds with love.

The heart understands and forgives others, and refuses to stop loving another human being, even when their negative actions can no longer be suffered or tolerated. The heart continues to love even when involvement becomes too difficult. In short, the human heart is the vessel that facilitates the realization of our highest self. It is the very center of love in our lives and following its prompts will enrich our lives in immeasurable ways.

The heart is where real love lies, whereas love's counterfeit currency, ego love, is a product of the mind. There is a big difference between ego love and real love. Ego love wants our partners to be a certain way, to fulfill some of our needs, to bolster our ego by having certain attributes that they bring to a relationship. Ego love is pleased by the fact that you are famous or wealthy. Ego love believes that our relationship is good when you are totally committed to me and you do not express emotions or feelings destructive to our relationship. Ego love starts to make me feel confused about you when I see your weaknesses. Ego love cares how acceptable you are to my friends and family.

Ego love says that I may feel embarrassed at times to be with you, and in some circumstances. Ego love hides behind dishonesty and will not share with you real feelings or disclose some actions for fear that it will hurt our relationship. Ego love feels intense jealousy when others are involved in your life. Ego love will remain in the relationship because of need, despite your destructive actions. Ego love says that you must do a lot for me to justify my loving you. Ego love does a lot for you, but in the back of its mind always expects some return.

Real love, however, accepts and loves unconditionally. Real love seeks the person beyond the images, the masks, and the outer appearance. Real love seeks the inner person and then shows that person unconditional love and acceptance. It says I like and respect who you are inside. Real love understands why you do things that are not always in your, or our, best interest, and feels compassionate towards you. Real love wants to help you overcome your weaknesses.

Real love believes that outer images are not necessary for me to feel close to you or want to give you my love. Real love says that it is okay, indeed it is preferable, for me to see your weaknesses, so I can help support you. Real love does not care if you are wealthy, smart, well-dressed, socially acceptable, or always strong. Real love does not react to others in your life with jealousy, but, rather, allows you the space to decide who you want to be.

Real love gives to you and will feel good about giving to you regardless of whether you give back. Real love acts honestly and forthrightly, even if that means the relationship may suffer or end. Real love never attempts to control you. Real love says that you always deserve my love, for you are as worthy as anyone to receive it.

Real love loves you for love's sake, not mine.

16.

In the end, love is everything. The real value of our lives is the measure by which we have learned to love.

In your own quest for real love, how much time do you spend making love a priority in your life. How much time do you spend developing rituals of love? Do you think about love consciously every day? Do you set achievable goals to demonstrate loving action daily? Do you examine your actions and reactions every day to determine whether the way you act or react is really who you are and who you want to be?

So many of us seem to exist day to day, almost robotically, seemingly not conscious that each and every moment we are choosing to love or not. Unless you become consciously aware of the issue of love, love cannot become a priority in your life. Unless you become aware of kindness and charity, these things will not be strong influences in your life. Unless you become aware of the feelings of your partner, you will not be sensitive to what he or she is experiencing. In sum, you must become aware of that which you wish to become. It will not happen automatically.

Seasoned athletes appear to compete at a professional level almost instinctively, but in reality they have practiced and honed their skills for years and years on a daily basis. If we want to become experts at love, then we must be prepared to make it a conscious priority in our lives and practice it on a daily basis. Only then will the art and practice of loving become habitual, making us appear to love almost effortlessly.

People often claim to have love as a major priority, but then do nothing to nurture loving feelings, thoughts and actions in their lives. We spend many hours a day at work, at play, and at rest. But how many hours a day do we spend developing love in our lives? How much do we read or learn about love? How much time do we spend thinking about loving actions and practicing them? Unless we can say that we spend time **each day** focused on these types of activities, how can love be a priority in our lives?

Many of us think of ourselves as loving individuals for we have loving motivations, desires and intentions. But how many of us consciously put effort towards demonstrating to others our loving feelings and intentions? Loving comes from doing and being, not just from feeling. Every day we are presented with countless opportunities to make love a priority in our lives and to act in a loving way. We must begin to consciously make love a priority and begin to capitalize on opportunities to love.

Choose to love always, in all situations, even if your "natural reaction" would be to act or react differently. The next time you feel like reacting negatively to a situation, stop for a moment, take note of how you are feeling, and then choose to react with love. See how it makes you feel to love in the face of adversity. Focus on the feelings you experience as you rise above a negative situation and take the higher ground. Recognize and acknowledge the feelings of peace and joy that result, and appreciate yourself for reacting in a loving way.

It is in these moments that you will begin to see what God has in mind for us.

Life, you see, is all about love; it is not about one day going to heaven, it is about creating heaven today. Life is not about one day being able to live with God, it is about becoming and realizing the part of God that exists in you. Choose each and every day, therefore, in every circumstance, to act and react in love. For in the end, love is everything, the all.

The sum value of our lives is not counted by the degree to

which we succeed at work, the amount of education we receive, or the amount of money or possessions we accumulate. All of these are temporal indicators that only demonstrate our commitment to their acquisition.

The real value of our lives is the measure by which we have learned to love.

Part Four.

The End, The Beginning, The All

1.

The infinite strength of spirit and soul is the property of all.

Picture if you will looking through a small hole in a screen and seeing a glimpse of beautiful scenery outside. As you spend more and more time looking out of the hole, imagine that it slowly begins to grow in size. As it grows larger and larger, more and more of the scenery outside comes into view. Soon the screen disappears completely and you find that you have become a part of the scenery.

The scenery outside is like the universal soul, and the screen is that which blocks our view, our touch of the soul. There are special moments in our lives when tiny holes appear through which you and I can catch a glimpse of the soul. The more time we spend trying to see through these holes, the larger and more frequent they become and you and I will see more and more of what lies beyond the screen. When we learn to clear that which continually blocks our view of the soul, the screen will vanish and we will become one with the soul. This scenery, this soul, exists in everyone. In some it is manifested more than others. But it exists in everyone.

That is why to believe or say that one is superior to another has no meaning to the soul. To say that man is superior to animals or plants has no meaning, for the whole universe is one and the soul of each is the soul of all. All of our struggles, pains, pleasures, tears, smiles, and all that we do and think should move us towards tearing up the screen, making the hole bigger, thinning the layers that remain between us and the complete manifestation of our divine soul. Our work is to rid ourselves of those things that prevent us from seeing and feeling the universal soul that flows through all things.

The sun is covered by layers of clouds, but remains unaffected by them. The work of the wind is to drive the clouds away. The more the clouds disappear, the more the light of the sun appears. Like the sun, the soul is always there – it is always infinite, absolute, and eternal. It only becomes clouded at times by our weaknesses, our judgments, and our misunderstandings.

The purpose of this book, and ultimately the work you are doing by reading it, is to be like the wind, to drive some of the clouds that block your view of the sun, the universal soul. That is the purpose of the Law of Self Realization: to help develop the happiness, peace and love that result from a recognition of the true nature of the soul and the divinity that exists within you. You may or may not know this divinity.

We live in a world that feeds on insecurity and our unhealthy desire for outside stimuli - be it power, money, sex, or some other pleasure distraction. Searching for these things, the unhappy person fills their need for security and love momentarily, until the novelty of the pleasure wears off and the hole in the heart and soul re-emerges. This strategy we are taught is a lot like feeding a hungry man with fish. The fish satisfies for a short time, but it is not long until the hunger returns and again more fish must be found to feed. Following the principles outlined in this book, however, teaches one to fill the hunger from within, to remove the hunger. This results in real satisfaction, real happiness, and less need for pleasure distractions or power games.

When we chase ambition, power, sex and money in insecure ways, without a deep awareness of what causes us to act or react in a particular way, or when we respond emotionally with upset or anger to circumstances or people that do not please us, it is because we have not learned to fill our own souls, to satisfy our own hunger. When we act in these ways, it is like we are searching for fish to eat. We like to lay blame on others for our hunger and for the things in our lives that disappoint us or cause us pain. However, the people and circumstances of our lives are no more responsible for this pain, than is the fish that would get put on our plate for dinner responsible for our hunger. We alone are responsible.

Once we learn to remove our hunger and satisfy our needs from within, then we become free to remove our hooks from the water. Rather than become an object for us to devour and eat, the fish, then, become objects for us to appreciate and admire. Likewise, once we satisfy our hunger from within we become free to be happy, to appreciate the life that surrounds us, and to give love freely to others. People, things and circumstances that once were devoured to distract us from our own pain, now become objects of our gratitude, kindness and love.

Finding yourself allows you to begin sharing your gifts and your light with others. Everyone has unique talents and gifts that can bring great benefits to others. That is the glory of our physical separation from the whole. It allows us to bring our diverse and unique gifts to others, to help them recognize their own divinity, their own godliness, and their own souls. It also helps us show others their connection to the whole, despite their physical separation or diversity.

Deriving unity from diversity and variety is the plan of nature. In all species, unity is found within the characteristics and traits of individuals. Although each individual is different than the next in some small way, taken together these individuals have unified characteristics and purpose.

This lesson from nature can also be applied to our spiritual experience. You may observe that some religions adhere to fixed doctrines and do their best to persuade their members and others to adopt them unconditionally and obediently. They place before society only one coat that must fit everyone equally. But the real glory of spiritual existence is the unity that is derived from the diversity and variety of spiritual experience. The individual differences of spiritual or religious experience are not important. Rather, it is the unifying principles of love, service, charity, etc., that spring from our differences that reflect the true nature of God.

All of our differences, all of our distinctions, all of our doctrines, teachings and principles that appear so seemingly different, are collectively nothing more than tools that allow us to chisel away the layers that cloak our true selves, our eternal cores, our own divinity. These apparent differences are simply representations of different dreams and manifestations of belief in a spiritual core that is the same for all. Let all these variations remain eternally, therefore, for they are the eternal play of life.

You may be wealthy and I may be poor; you may be strong and I may be weak; you may be educated and I may be ignorant; you may manifest spirit and I perhaps less so. But so what? Let us have these differences. They are the glory and challenges of our physical existence. But because you are physically or intellectually stronger than I am, you should not feel superior to me. Because you have more wealth than me, is no reason why you should be considered greater than me. Because it is easier to see God in you, is no reason for you to be accepted and loved while I am not. The soul that exists in you and me is the same, in spite of the differences.

Our eternal objective is not to destroy variation in the conditions of life, but rather to recognize unity in spite of these variations. To recognize that God exists in each of us regardless of our condition, differences, or fears. As we learn to balance body, mind and spirit, lose expectation, develop our purpose, and grow in wisdom and love, so too will we acknowledge and recognize that the infinite strength of the soul is the property of all – despite our apparent weaknesses.

2.

The true path to happiness and enlightenment is found by following your own heart and doing so even though others do not follow or even understand your direction.

Deepak Chopra, the noted writer and teacher, teaches that in the end, our separate and distinct lives can be likened unto a single drop of rain that falls from the heavens from which we came. We arrive on this earth to provide nourishment and sustenance to everything we touch. We collect and become like a river with those that are like us. As we flow freely together, we ultimately form currents that will, following the course of nature, fall into a hollow where a whirlpool is made. The whirlpool represents our world of space, time and causation and our struggle to define ourselves.

Each drop is required to go through this whirlpool so that, one day, it can emerge again in the form of a free current. For some, the time in the whirlpool is long, because being attracted to the elements found therein, they are sucked deep within and languish there a great time. Others, recognizing the restricting elements of the whirlpool and the lack of freedom that exists within it, move to the outside and as a result stay but a little while. Ultimately, they are once again set free to run their own course through nature. They become free to define who they are and what they are. This is the purpose of life, the reason for our existence.

Sooner or later something will call you to a particular path. You may recognize this "something" as single moment, and urge, a fascination or a peculiar turn of events. But whatever it is, by following the principles in this book, you will begin to recognize it as an announcement: **"This is what I must do, this is who I am."** For some, it will be a return to familiar ground, somewhere they have already been. As T.S. Eliot once said: "The end of all our exploring will be to arrive where we started and to know the place for the first time." For others, it will feel like a new voyage, a new discovery. Becoming who they really are for these people will be like exploring uncharted territory. For these the words of Andre Gide will ring true: "One doesn't discover new lands without consenting to lose sight of the shore for a very long time." It will be frightening, it will be scary, but at a soul level they will know it is right and they will be drawn to these new experiences like metal to a magnet.

Whatever the path, whatever the experience, the secret is in letting go of the fear and following your heart. Listen to your inner voice and learn quickly to embrace who it is you are and want to be. Let the world hear your music. As Oliver Wendell Holmes once declared, too many of us "go to our graves with our music still inside."

3.

Principles of Being.

This is not the end of our journey together, it is the beginning. I am committed to helping you find your way. I want to help you find your music and learn to play it. Loudly.

One thing I believe will help you on your path is to create

a priority list of what you value, who you are, and what you stand for. These should be principles that guide you to becoming everything you envision for yourself. They should be that which reflects the highest choices you would make for yourself. Choose these values wisely and carefully. Make sure they really represent you. Wear them as your badge of honor. They should be principles you are happy to have the whole world associate with you. Carry these principles with you wherever you go and share them with anyone you believe will benefit. Each and every day make it a part of your consciousness to evaluate yourself against these values, and change them if they no longer reflect who you are. But be them, in all that you do, until they become your total reality.

I offer you my guiding principles. My principles of being. They are the principles that underscore the Law of Self Realization and ultimately are those that I believe lead to greater happiness and love. They are my **"*soul matters.*"** They are not meant to guide anyone but me, but perhaps from them I can help you find your way.

Principles of Being

I acknowledge that every circumstance and relationship in my life is a direct or indirect result of choices I have made, or failed to make. I understand that I am the supreme creator of my life and everything in it, and I choose every day to accept my present circumstances and relationships exactly as they are, unless I am consciously acting to change them.

I believe that life is exactly as we choose to see it. All people, places and things can present both a negative and positive perspective. We, as observers, make the choice of what we see. Because I want to fill my life with joy, I choose to recognize beauty in all things.

I will try to have every choice I make be consistent with the highest vision I have of myself. Rather than try to control or manipulate others to conform to my addictive behaviors or programming, I will allow others to simply be, and will learn to change my addictions into preferences. I know this is the only way I can be truly happy.

I know it is better to live my life without expectations or attachment to results. Although I may plan for the future, I must not become too attached to the fulfillment of those plans or I may miss other more fulfilling opportunities. If life takes me in a direction different than the one I have planned, I believe it is for my ultimate good.

I want to approach each and every moment of every day with the same level of enthusiasm, happiness, passion and present-moment focus as I have making love. Life and everything in it, like physical love-making, is a wonderful experience that I know I must appreciate, using all of my senses to fully enjoy it.

Honesty is one of the single greatest principles in life, and I will approach every person, circumstance or situation with a commitment to be honest with myself, to openly and honestly present my true thoughts and feelings to others, and to never lie, deceive or mislead another person.

I believe in being sensitive, and before acting or reacting to any situation or person, I will try my best to act or react in a way that I would want to be treated under the same circumstances.

I cannot judge any person, situation or thing for I do not know all of the facts. My experience with anything is limited to my interaction with that person, situation or thing – and that is not the complete picture. Therefore, I cannot judge whether anything or anyone is good or bad, right or wrong. I also know I should not judge myself harshly, for I am a learning, loving human being that can draw strength from all of my experiences.

I recognize that I can only view life through my own rose-colored glasses, and the beliefs, opinions or standards of any group or person, including my own, are not necessarily universal truths.

I have a thirst and love for knowledge and understanding, and I recognize that true learning and growth comes only from effort, experience and a willingness to accept some new ideas, even if it means the rejection of previously-held beliefs.

I love living and I know that a healthy body is an essential part of maintaining the quality of my life experience. Consequently, I will exercise my body and will feed it with healthy air, food and drink. I will heal it and rest it when necessary, and I will treat my body with loving care. I will touch others and smile often, for it is my true nature to be kind. I will also laugh a lot.

I believe in God, Spirit, or the Soul – whatever name we give to that power in the universe that exists beyond our obvious senses. Life becomes magical when we see the clues that spirit offers and I will strive to find them. I also know that inviting Spirit into my life allows me to make better choices than I would otherwise make, for it allows me to view life from the perspective of heaven.

I believe that each of us can contribute to the world in some unique way. For me, it is to share with others the principles that I hold dear, in the hope that these principles will benefit others as much as they have given benefit to me. I am fulfilled and happy when I act in service to others.

The real purpose of life is love. Love is our very essence, the all which created us and is us. This day I will work to remove that which blocks my love from flowing freely. I will learn to love myself and I will liberally share my love with others. I will be kind, understanding and compassionate. I will make love a daily focus and priority in my life, and I will try to fill every moment of my life and yours with love. I will also tell you how much I love you.

I have not yet attained these principles, but I am trying to do it. I may never totally achieve them, but you may achieve yours. So try! Learn what you may from me, open your eyes with the light that I offer, but learn to walk for yourself.

No one but you can play your music and you cannot genuinely play the music of another. You must find your own music, your own path, and your own adventure. To do this, you must of course find yourself first. Then, the only question becomes whether or not you will say yes to your adventure and to playing your music.

As a child we learn from parents and others and we grow by mimicking their behavior. Ultimately, however, we do not grow up and become ourselves until we transform their thoughts into our own experiences. Until we become our own person, modifying what we have learned from others, we do not become or realize our greater selves.

It is my sincere desire, hope, and prayer that this book will help you find your music, help you find your path. Do not wait for others to follow and do not expect that others will understand. They have their own paths to follow and their own music to play. If they truly love you, they will be there to support you regardless of the path you choose.

Along the way you will find other books to help you, other teachers to teach you. As you continue your journey, however, remember the words of Henry Miller: "No man is great enough or wise enough for any of us to surrender our destiny to. The only way in which anyone can lead us is to restore to us the belief in our own guidance." Nothing other than your own experiences will teach you how divine you really are. Nothing other than walking down your own path will unlock the keys of heaven that lie waiting inside you.

Do not be afraid, you cannot make a mistake. All paths lead to the same place.

Do not be afraid – I will be there ... not behind you, or in front of you, but beside you making my own way.

As we walk along together we can look out for each other and help each other.

I will be there for you.

And you for me.

And together we will realize our divinity . . . .

ABOUT THE AUTHOR

After graduating with honors from law school in 1989, Austin went to work as a trial lawyer for one of the largest law firms in the world, where he represented numerous Fortune 500 companies. He then put his skills to work for one of the oldest Fortune 100 companies of America, where he ultimately served both as General Counsel and as a senior executive of a European division, based in London, England. At the age of 37, Austin resigned his position at the top of his business career to pursue his passion for changing people's lives.

Throughout his life Austin has been an avid student of spirituality, philosophy, psychology, and the mind, body and spirit movement. He has participated in and won awards for numerous Pro Bono and volunteer activities, including work for the homeless, the United States Senate, the California State Bar, and service as a missionary in Chile, South America. He has been featured as a speaker at the International Mind, Body & Spirit Festival in London, England.

Austin currently writes, speaks and teaches internationally in the fields of spirituality, relationship dynamics, and life strategy and management. He is the founder and President of Quantum Horizons, LLC, a company dedicated to guiding the development and vision of people and organizations.

You can contact Austin and learn more about his workshops, lectures and his personal coaching programs by visiting him online at www.austinvickers.com, by calling the following number: (480) 491-5591, or by writing to him at the following address: 1730 E. Warner Road, Suite 10-142, Tempe, Arizona, 85284.